Imaginings of an Infovore

*

The Further Musings

of

Raymond R. A. Burke

ISBN: 978-1-9162746-3-1

This book was set in Adobe Garamond Pro

Geek, Batman cosplayer, and wannabe Iceland explorer - Raymond Burke is a British-born author. His background includes a teenaged life in Canada and the US, his twenties in the British Army as an aircraft technician, his thirties as a mature archaeology student with BSc and MSc degrees from University College London, and from his forties a sci-fi author. He is also a member of The Mars Society.

Raymond cunningly lives without a fridge, satellite TV, iPods, and he also can't drive. And while he has taken up 3D printing, he's a self-confessed 21st century caveman - and loves it!

Through all, he has been a keen writer. He lives in London.

ACKNOWLEDGMENTS

Following on from my first volume, *Musings of an Infovore*, I would like to say a big thank you to Helium.com, the writing site which gave me the opportunity to express my thoughts and ideas during a downturn in my life. To Mark Ranalli, President & CEO of Helium and all the senior staff who helped me along the way, listened to ideas, and had the belief in me to manage the Arts & Humanities Channel. To the stewards I managed and who made life at Helium fun and informative. And of course to my fellow Helium writers who enlightened and entertained me.

My writing wasn't formed in a vacuum, nor just from my time writing essays at university, but mostly from my formative years at schools and experiences growing up in other countries and in various employments. So a big thank you to my teachers, supervisors, colleagues, fellow students and friends who inspired me along my writing journey.

And my sincerest gratitude to those who have allowed me to contribute their correspondence to this work: David Dugan, former CEO of Windfall Films and to Bruno Comby, President of the Environmentalists for Nuclear Energy.

Cover design by Ennel John Espanola and Janet Dado (DPI Printing Solutions).

Formatting by Catherine Entero.

To

My parents

Contents

INTRODUCTION

As chronicled more fully in my book *Musings of an Infovore*, in 2007-08, I was unemployed for roughly eight months, having completed my MSc in Archaeology in 2006 and left the security industry the following year. While I lazily looked for new work, I somehow came across and joined an online writing site, Helium, in early December 2007. There you could publish your articles on a variety of subjects, rate other articles, participate in debates, make money.

I had already started writing my sci-fi novel (almost 30 years in the making and then some), written essays and dissertations at university, and also songs and poems in my spare time, but I hadn't really written articles with the hope of earning money, so here was my chance.

From that time onward, I wrote over 230 articles on a multitude of subjects. It was a very creative time for me even after I started working again. I finished my sci-fi novel in 2010 (self-published in 2012) and continued to write articles for the website until 2011, when I decided to call it quits due to my work commitments.

While the first volume of my Infovore book series focused on the more serious articles and essays, this second volume concentrates on the articles about entertainment, a couple dozen songs and poems I crafted, a couple of ambitious unrealised projects, and the couple score proposed TV shows I created before and after this same time. This latter endeavour led me to try to break into the TV industry. And though that creative spirit hasn't left me, these volumes of work were lifelines during darker times. I'm proud to share them here.

As with the essays and articles in the first volume, I will have brief notes for some of the works as to why they were written and other random thoughts. Except the poems; they never need explaining, especially the tomes of the lovelorn. Most of the poems and songs were also uploaded to the Helium site and have the sub-channel titles included and my own title below.

I hope you find my ideas and themes thoughtful and maybe inspire you to write your own essays, poems, songs, TV ideas, or even a book. Creativity is an enduring source of happiness for an Infovore.

Ray Burke
October 2020

Entertainment

16/Jan/2008

Arts & Humanities - Comic Books & Graphic Novels
Comic Books: Marvel Universe Versus the DC Universe

Superhero Icons

2020 vision
I used to be a big comic book collector before selling off my collection around 2007-08. The first comic book I bought was DC's Star Trek #18, while I lived in Toronto, 1985. When our family moved to Brooklyn, New York in 1986, my favourite comic book shop was just off Flatbush and Utica Avenues, quite a walk away from home at the time. And of course the famous Forbidden Planet in Manhattan was a subway ride away. I started out with Marvel (X-Men, Alpha Flight, The Defenders, etc) then later 'graduated' to DC comics with Justice League. Nowadays, I don't think I could keep up with all the different iterations and reboots of sueprheroes. It's a vast universe, or indeed, multiverse of comic books out there and long may they continue.

Why have some comic book characters remained more durable than others? For seven decades DC comics has sustained the market for their characters, reinventing them for modern times, while their biggest competitor, Marvel, has been bringing gritty realism for fifty years in its modern incarnation. The Big Two have survived imitators, financial battles, market slumps, and creative differences, and are now thriving in their industries in print, celluloid and digital forms, not to mention merchandising. Even with the best writers, artists, management, and legions of fans there seems to be some underlying reason why these characters have emerged as global icons. Below is a generalised view of the DC and Marvel universes, there are exceptions and other heroes to consider, but I believe that this overview is enough for the space provided.

In the DC universe you have the big seven: Superman, Batman, Wonder Woman, Martian Manhunter, Aquaman, The Flash and Green Lantern. They are regarded as god-like figures and even convene on the moon, or satellites, or remote locations akin to Mount Olympus. They are remote figures, a rarefied breed; they are the modern day archetypes of ancient Gods:

Superman is the sun God; man of strength, speed, intelligence and compassion. Wonder Woman is the embodiment of the female warrior and mother earth goddess. Batman is the philosopher/soldier; an Ares, or mortal Achilles, warrior, leader, and tyrannical. The Flash is the messenger of the Gods and Aquaman –king of the seas. Martian Manhunter is the shape shifter; the Coyote or Loki; wise, enigmatic, an outsider. Green Lantern is Odysseus; loyal warrior, thinker and daring wanderer.

The popularity of the DC characters could be explained by their timeless qualities. They could be any of the various mythical Gods and heroes found around the world from the beginning of time. Even the DC world is more unreal and weird compared to ours with the main threats to Earth being from outer space, yet the heroes try not intercede within national or international affairs, if they do not involve super-powered beings, wanting 'humans' to run their own affairs instead. The nature of the characters' powers is also different. They are metahumans, intentionally created or enhanced, or have alien heritages or alien-endowed powers. Their secret identities are usually high-profile jobs or they are billionaires or bankrolled by them. They seemed to be compelled to be heroes out of righteous justice from personal histories or societal demands, stemming from a lofty idealism.

In Marvel the direct correlation to DC's big seven is the newly formed Illuminati. They are Iron Man founder of the Avengers, Doctor Strange – sorcerer supreme, Mr. Fantastic of the Fantastic 4, Namor the Sub-Mariner, Charles Xavier leader of the X-men and Black Bolt -king of the Inhumans. They command the world's most powerful groups and the leaders gather together every so often to decide how the world should be run. The Illuminati are the power in the shadows, the council of kings, warriors and shamans, and of the elders from ages past.

The Marvel universe is one of the every-day men with extraordinary powers (e.g. Spider-Man, Hulk, Daredevil). Their teams, families and friends live and work together in schools, mansions, towers and houses among the people. They are more demigods than DC Gods able to relate to ordinary people, because they are one of them. They have real jobs and concerns for family.

Marvel's mutants are the persecuted underclass of superhero-dom, though they are scientists, teachers, ex-soldiers, and kings. Their world is more ground level, more political in nature and in making. The nature of their power is in their genes, usually from birth or accidentally gained. If DC's heroes were meant to be great, then Marvel's heroes have had greatness thrust upon them; the reluctant heroes, the outcasts and the unseen. They fight for survival and their ideals are murkier and blurred so that the anti-hero seems the norm (The Punisher, Wolverine, Magneto).

Whose world would I rather live in? DC heroes tend to attract bigger threats, but leave the common man alone; their concerns are global, galactic and universal. Marvel heroes are less space-oriented and concentrate at street level where one may get caught in the cross-fire. DC heroes are more in the open, though the Justice League, Justice Society, Teen Titans, *et al* seem to avoid press paparazzi, while Marvel's heroes, the X-Men, X-Factor, Fantastic 4 and The Avengers are a mixed group of camera shy and attention seeking super-celebrities. DC heroes do not usually mix business with pleasure and while a few are politically inclined, the world is basically run by 'humans'. Marvel has mutant rights and mutant policy makers that have changed the world's views on 'human' rights. Marvel's world is also more cosmopolitan, earthy and sociable. They live almost normal lives, go home, sleep, work and save the world because no one else will. But DC's seemingly sterile and inaccessible superhero community appeals more to me, however. Their deeds would be on the news, but they would not be in your face all the time, like some over-hyped celebrity. They seem to be always on the job in a never-ceasing mission to safeguard the world. They constantly shine, like the stars and the Gods who made them.

So I hope this quick and general guide has helped. There is so much more to uncover and consider. The world of comic books is a wonderful world to ponder and envision and long may they continue.

17/Jan/2008

Entertainment - Entertainment (Other)
Most Powerful Superheroes

Most Powerful Superhero – Let's Hear it for the Girls

2020 vision
I prefer the comic book version of Carol Danver's Ms Marvel to the recent film version. Of course they'll flesh out the film role, but there was something missing. Danver's comic book charisma and leadership qualities of the Avengers following the 'Civil War' saga was lacking from the character in the film. Maybe that will change as it would be a shame to miss out on such a great iconic character.

As a guy there are many superheroes that have graced the comic book pages with their supreme abilities, but I have chosen to go with a superheroine that has really impressed me over the past year and that is Carol Danvers: Ms. Marvel.

Ms. Marvel is in the Superman class of power and a powerful icon. As Ms. Marvel she is invulnerable, can fly and also fire energy blasts. Danvers is also vastly experienced as an Air Force officer and pilot, CIA agent, and space adventurer as Binary with the Starjammers. She has proven herself without her powers, which adds to her superhero profile.

She is now the First Lady of Marvel and in a league of her own and greatly deserving of the resurrection she has received. Lately, the leader of the Mighty Avengers, trainer of the next generation of Avengers, and wary of Iron Man's agendas, Ms. Marvel is smart, sassy, likeable, approachable and a real woman. She's possibly the first hero to have a blog of their adventures. Few heroes of her class within the Marvel Universe seem to be able to hold their own when all around them has irrevocably broken down.

Ms. Marvel has no peers, with Jean Grey's Phoenix, the Scarlet Witch, maybe Storm, and possibly Rogue who stole her abilities, comparing in power, but without the leadership, flair and panache. Compared to DC there is Wonder Woman, Mary Marvel, Power Girl and Supergirl (though the latter two are technically the same person). Ms. Marvel could seriously replace Wonder Woman in a trinity of Superman, Ms. Marvel and

Batman. She is much more talented and dynamic than the boring and underused Wonder Man and more than a match for Nick Fury.

The Writer, Brian Reed, and artist, Roberto De La Torre have done a fantastic job of re-introducing Carol Danvers to a new audience (in 2006) and putting her right back in the major leagues of heroes as the Best of the Best. Sure she has a sexy costume, but the intelligence of the writing and her ability to handle global crises elevates her above the bimbo in high heels status. Her adventures are probably the only ones I would buy with a female lead.

Ms. Marvel may not be as powerful as Superman, as intelligent as Batman or Mr. Fantastic, as popular as Spider-Man, as fearsome as Wolverine, or a symbol of freedom like Captain America, but Ms. Marvel embodies these traits and more, more so because she is a woman holding her own in super-dangerous universe. Ms. Marvel compares to Wonder Woman, the only other female lead who commands respect and offers alternative leadership, though of course Wonder Woman is a Goddess, while Danvers is a human with Kree-endowed powers.

In the male-dominated world of comic books, Ms. Marvel, is a superheroine who could easily be the world-class leader and protector that Superman is in DC. She can do this solo or with premier groups like The Avengers. As a role model, Ms. Marvel offers an alternative for female readers, redresses the balance of powerful female heroes, has a positive influence overcoming difficulties and regaining her place in the top tier. Well done, Ms. Marvel –I salute you.

17/Jan/2008

Entertainment - TV Genres & Trends
Speculation on what a comic book TV show should include

Comic Book Weekly

2020 vision
I actually did try to turn this idea into a TV show sending it to various production companies, without success, as chronicled below in the Ray TV section.

I have always wanted to see a proper and dedicated show about comic books on TV. So I have tried to put together my version of a show that will examine the enduring popularity of the comic book on world culture.

The Introduction will be: 'Why do superheroes matter in this day and age? Do they? Are they modern-day equivalents to the old gods or heroes of the future? Do they represent something within ourselves today? Comic Book Weekly will take a timely, if somewhat irreverent peek into the world of the superheroes.'

The structure of the show will be a half-hour programme, each week delving into comic books and spin-off graphic novels, films, television shows, merchandising, books, conventions, computer games and many more incarnations of comic book heroes via interviews, shop visits, emails, competitions, etc. My show should be successful because it deals exclusively with this genre, while other shows (e.g. news clips, film specials, etc) focus on it short-term when a comic book becomes a film adaptation. Comic Book Weekly will be a constant and accessible source of information without resorting to repeated satellite shows, the Internet or quickly out-of-date magazines.

The people behind the scenes: writers, artists, inkers, letterers, et al and the actors who breathe life into these heroes will also be featured. The Legends' Corner will recall writers and artists from the past who contributed to the wealth of the genre. The works of DC Comics, Image, Homage, Marvel, 2000 AD and others will reveal what it takes to be successful and how to create and perpetuate enduring characters. Competitions could also be held to find and/or appreciate new writers and artists.

The impact of superhero television series, both live and animated, has boosted the aura of the comic book world, even though the comic book itself was in decline for a time. The rise of women and minority comic book characters are on the increase with an Indian version of Spider-Man and a Middle Eastern super-group planned. Light-hearted discussions with anthropologists and psychologists could also analyse the superhero 'psyche', the media frenzy superheroes would cause in our world, other effects on our culture and the worldwide fandom phenomena.

Meanwhile...with the popularity of *Heroes*, the Batman, Superman and Spider-Man films, Comic Book Weekly will appeal to adults, who clog the comic books shops buying for themselves and their children, and also to children who love comic books and want to experience alternative reading and entertainment. My show would represent the chance to be both enthralled by the heroics of superheroes and also to look within ourselves and see those heroes reflected back.

07/Feb/2008

Entertainment - Movie Genres
Examining the mythology and themes of Westerns

Why I Love Westerns

No other country has a history such as the Wild West of America. It was a country of wildness that needed to be tamed, of confrontations with Native Americans, of ambiguous law and order, rickety towns and triumph in adversity. Westerns have familiar themes running through them that forever draw me to them. The Western goes right back to Colonial times, when the young independent America was fighting off combinations of British, French or Indian forces. As soon as the traditional Colonial soldiers uniforms disappeared and the buckskins were pulled on in pursuit of the frontier, the Western was born.

The Story:
The story usually begins with Pioneers, lazy green-horn, Eastern city-folk drawn to the west to build new towns, establish fortunes, or to seek a cure for illness in the dry West. In the wagon train there's usually at least one law-abiding man, one trouble-making man, a lady of disputed honour, a lawyer/priest/doctor, a no-nonsense businessman, a suffering family and a single woman looking for an honest man, but can't make up her mind about the trouble-maker. There's also the old, crotchety, long-whiskered cook/tradesman with a sense of humour and a bottle of whiskey. The trail was character-building, not all made it, and those who did became a tightly-knit founding group. These were usually the hallmarks of any Western town once the pioneers became settled.

Horsemanship:
One of the most fascinating aspects of the Western is the relationship between man and horse. The skills, training, and experience needed to perform some of the action scenes were phenomenal. The stunt work was incredible with shooting, roping, falling, jumping, fighting and any other exploit on a horse, especially at full gallop. This enshrined the unit of one man and his horse as a classic Western image. As I express below, the actors/stuntmen were usually in multiple Westerns and knew how to ride naturally, as opposed to modern actors. They were veteran, saddle-ready, weather-beaten, bean-eating actor/cowboys who probably could have survived in the Old West by wit alone.

The Mystery Man:
The Man with no Name, the wandering stranger, the impersonator, the mistaken identity, and the man with a mysterious past are all staples of Westerns. The major theme of Westerns was revenge and redemption. Would they be good or bad? Who could draw the fastest? We watched heartless outlaws redeem themselves heroically and good men turn outlaw for revenge only to give up the gun in the end, in a choice between being good or bad. A lone man (with his horse) entering town was usually viewed with suspicion and he had to prove himself one way or another. It was every man for himself, you either had to stand up for yourself or be rode roughshod over. More than any other film genre, Westerns were all about the character of a man. And upon these men, America was built.

Romance and Womenfolk:
Love was quick to bloom in a Western. No sooner had a man and a young starlet clapped eyes on each other, then there was swooning and a-courting on the horizon. Even if there was no overt sexuality or gestures to that effect, by the end of the film, the cowboy had a willing wife-to-be and ranch waiting for him. There was also a woman's choice between the outlaw and the good guy and if she made the wrong choice, it was usually her who paid the price. Women were generally portrayed as strong pioneering wives, femme fatales or swooning tomboy cowgirls who blossomed into young ladies.

The Cavalry:
The sight of the Cavalry uniform is a stirring occasion, an instantly recognisable symbol of the West. Forever associated with the bugle-rallying, last-minute rescue, the Cavalry was a force for both good and ill when dealing with Indian uprisings and settling the West. Their forts were either defensive settlements or intrusive staging posts for more white man destruction. As with any Western element, they had both good and bad Commanders, soldiers and representatives, but they symbolised the advancing march of law and order, civilisation and the American way.

Bar fights and Shootouts:
Marshalls, sheriffs, Pinkerton Detectives, Texas Rangers, militias, Posses, lynch mobs, outlaws, cowboys, ranch hands and gunmen were always engaged in shootouts and disputes. Gunplay and fancy shooting has always excited the crowds and there was even a duel between a harpoon and a gun in 'Terror in a Texas Town'. Quick draws, mass shoot outs and

circled wagons waiting for the cavalry are such great spectacles, but bar fights as in 'Dodge City' with guns and fists flying in equal measure could be just as enjoyable.

Cattlemen versus Farmers:
One of the biggest battles was between Ranchers and Farmers; the cattlemen and the sheep herders and the rights to water, land and supplies. These two camps were usually family orientated with their values and lives at stake so they fended for themselves in endless feuds. They were laws unto themselves and winner took all. Watching such battles unfold really brought home that some communities were totally on their own and at the mercy of natural and man-made storms. Though they were ruthless, they were supplying food to other Westerners and the cities back east, so to them, livestock was an issue of life and death and they had to protect their land from all-comers.

Indians and Mexicans:
The enemies of the Westerners were usually Indians and Mexican bandits. Over time the Native Americans were seen in a better light and were not always the unjustified marauding savages, but proud defenders of their lands from the encroaching white man. Settlers were seen at their worst as gold-greedy, racist antagonists who tricked and stole to provoke conflict with the Native Americans. As for the Mexicans, they were usually bandits and revolutionaries ready to double-cross and start wars. Both peoples are hard done by in Westerns, though some revisionist Westerns tried to redress this imbalance. In the end, noble Indians and Mexican peasant Generals usually got the better of the corrupt Pale Face/gringo.

Humour:
This is an important element of the Western, whether intended or through the situation. Cowboying could be a funny business and there was plenty of humour on tap, usually from the old Cow Pokes who knew a wise word or two. Snappy dialogue or contemplations on life always brought out the best one-liners, wise-cracks or funny observations even while under fire. Humour was integral to the Western for making the best of a bad situation, with a light song, a harmonica, a fiddle or guitar to liven up the mood after a long day's ride. It also helped mitigate the true violent nature of Westerns with a smile of humanity.

Actors:
Though they are a product of their times, the actors were always convincing as their characters. You got the feeling that the actors, especially the ubiquitous supporting actors, could actually ride, shoot, hunt and trap game, live in the rough, build log cabins and towns, play the bar's piano and take on a cattle drive. While you couldn't be a cowboy yourself, the familiarity and knowledge imparted about Western life was both consciously and subliminally implanted in the mind and you felt the urge to be a part of the Western adventure. Today's actors film over leisurely months, stay in their luxurious trailers, can't ride a horse properly, or act as a believable cowboy. It's all about gun play and action without a decent story. Only a few modern Westerns have managed to buck this trend and capture the essence of the West, because they have starred actors who believed in and understood Westerns.

The Western usually ends just around World War I, with new-fangled automobiles on the scene and the cowboys absconding to Mexico to fight revolutions. The west became gentrified and ranchers, farmers and cowboys found themselves in a new world. The Wild West is still there, in rodeos, ranches and small desert towns, but modern cowboys now wear suits with cowboy boots, drive pickups and treat tourists to occasional cattle drives. Westerns may be on the wane at cinemas, but with a nostalgic back-catalogue the size of Texas, the Western will never fade into the sunset.

02/Mar/2008

Entertainment – Movie Genres
Top 20 vampire movies

My Top 10 Vampire Movies

I have always liked the vampire genre of films; some are quite bad, but others breaking new ground in tackling modern vampire issues while exploring and updating the origins and evolution of the vampires. There are a few films that do this and also a more eclectic collection of little known films. Here are my top ten:

1. Blade is one of the first major blockbusters and characters, from the comic books, to shine a light, as it were, on the vampire condition. Is there room for cohabitation or do humans and vampires have to constantly hunt each other? As a Daywalker, Blade, brilliantly played by Wesley Snipes, has the best of both worlds, though struggles with his vampire nature. Yes, this has all sorts of cultural parables, but it's a ripping yarn, both modern with Stephen Dorff's revolution of the vampire order, and traditional with the ancient families and their codes. An uneven trilogy does not tarnish the advancement of the vampire legends.

2. Underworld upped the ante on the portrayal of modern vampire cultures. Again, it's a blend of ultra-modern adventure as seen with the technological warfare against the werewolves and the traditional aristocratic families conducting themselves to ancient laws. Selene (Kate Beckinsale) is caught between the old way of life, leading the fight against the werewolves and then in her love for the hybrid, Michael. The sequel, Underworld-Evolution had a more epic feel to it and introduced a new, if somewhat contrived, origin to the vampire/werewolf mythology. Despite this, and with a third film possibly on the way, Underworld has brought the vampire into the 21st Century.

3. Near Dark (1987). A farm boy joins a tribe of southern vampire after falling for a girl who has infected him. I have a few memories of this film; a dark, wandering western-like film, but it also turns vampirism from a European or elitist tale into a home-grown American institution. Broke Back Vampire, anyone?

4. Ultraviolet (1998) –British TV mini-series. Jack Davenport's character accidentally stumbles across a secret government organisation working undercover within the police to hunt vampires, or 'Leeches' or 'Code 5' (Roman numeral V) as they are called. The Ultraviolet in this case is that most damaging part of sunlight. This was my first exposure to the notion of vampires as another human species who were attempting to modify their food source (us). I also liked the modern use of 'folkloric' weapons like ultraviolet beams and carbon bullets. Best quote: 'Our free range days are over.' British TV really hasn't touched the subject again.

5. Octane (2003). Madeline Stow is driving home on a late night with her rebellious teenage daughter (Mischa Barton) who runs off with a bizarre group of blood-letting psychos in a refitted fuel tanker, led by Jonathan Rhys Meyers. Again, vampires are implied, especially near the end, but it is a hypnotic trip of missing people, dreams, sex and violence. I rather enjoyed the ambiguity of the protagonists; were they vampires or just a bloody cult?

6. Thirst (1979). Chantal Contouri plays Kate Davis the descendant of a noble vampire house. She is abducted by a cult of would-be vampires who drink the blood of 'kept' slaves on their private farm. The blood is transferred, purified, and stored in vats. Kate, unaware of her 'nobility' is psychologically tortured into joining them and marrying another noble. This is probably one of the first films to deal with vampirism as a sub-sect of humanity. Again, it deals with purifying their food through technology, rituals of vampires and sexuality. Even with quaint effects and acting, there was a disturbing undertone in Kate's destiny to become a vampire. The will-she/won't she submit to the conditioning gleefully heaped upon her by the doctors was fantastic.

7. From Dusk Til Dawn (1996) is in a genre of its own; part crime thriller, part action-adventure, all comedy. George Clooney and Quentin Tarantino are murdering, robbing brothers who on the run, kidnap Harvey Keitel and his family and hole-up in a run down bar. Before you know it, the vampires, led by Salma Hayek, are feasting. It's gory fun from beginning to end

8/9. I wish I could highly recommend Lifeforce (1985) and Innocent Blood (1992). I know that I liked the films, they stand out in my lists of vampire films, yet I have not seen them recently to review their worthiness. But vampires from space and a family of mob vampires must be good. So I recommend them if only for the novelty of their stories.

10. Buffy the Vampire Slayer (1992). I am only including this film, because it introduced us to the later, and better, Buffy and Angel series. Without these rejuvenating series, I do not think that the genre would have evolved as it had. The stories of adventure, humour, pathos and 'humanity' were brilliantly imaged by Joss Whedon.

There are more, but these are my standouts, so curl up to late-night TV with your red wine and dodgy burgers. Fangs for the memories

14/Apr/2008

Entertainment – TV Genres & Trends
The Best British sci-fi TV shows

The TV Series UFO

While I love Doctor Who, its spin-offs Torchwood and the Sarah Jane Adventures, and the other Terry Nation series Blake's 7, one of my favourite British Sci-fi series was the short-lived 1970 show UFO. This was a Gerry and Sylvia Anderson production, creator of the Supermarionation programmes Thunderbirds, Stingray and Captain Scarlet, etc. UFO was set in the future (1980) and was about aliens invading Earth and abducting humans for nefarious purposes.

A secret organisation was established to deal with this threat: SHADO (Supreme Headquarters Alien Defence Organisation), which masqueraded as a movie studio in England led by Ed Straker, a former United States Air Force Colonel and astronaut. As with other Gerry Anderson productions, one of the best aspects of the show were the vehicles and spacecraft; top notch designs of sublime, yet unfeasible aerodynamics. My favourite were the Skydivers; a compact submarine with a sea/air fighter-craft attached to the front which was launched upon discovery of a UFO. Then there was the moonbase, which inexplicably had three silver-clad, purple-wigged girls at the 'reception/control'. It was glorious 1970s Anderson kitsch.

The combination of the adult elements in the storylines such as child death, sex and drugs, confused viewers feeling that the series was for children, but UFO was a dark-natured programme more suited for today's climate. After the second series, Anderson had proposed a revamped show- UFO: 1999, with more action set on an expanded moonbase. But it was rejected and Anderson created a new series from the ashes called- Space: 1999. Thus Moonbase Alpha, blasted from the moon on an inadvertent cosmic journey, was born. It is too bad that the somewhat superior UFO was discarded for another lost in space type-series, but with the current convention for resurrecting shows, UFO should be at the top of the list for a comeback.

Gerry Anderson should be more celebrated as the British Gene Roddenberry, his series have cemented themselves in the minds of children and adults all over the world. His far-sighted vision in both live-action and Supermarionation are still relevant today and could inspire and teach a few sci-fi makers today about creativity and action. UFO, is a worthy encounter of the third kind.

15/Apr/2008

Entertainment – TV Show Reviews
TV show reviews: Thunderbirds

5, 4, 3, 2, 1....Thunderbirds Are Go!

Thunderbirds, for me, is one of the most visionary TV programmes produced by Gerry and Sylvia Anderson, in 1965. International Rescue was born as former astronaut, Jeff Tracy, commanded his five sons, Scott, Virgil, John, Gordon and Alan in their high-tech missions and fantastical machines to save those in danger in 2065.

Their base was in their South Pacific island home. With Jeff as the base commander, Scott flew Thunderbird 1, the rapid response rocketplane; Virgil piloted the spectacularly ungainly, but essentially utilitarian Thunderbird 2, which was a 'fat green frog' with a removable belly section for replacement pods for specialised missions; Alan was the space pilot in Thunderbird 3, the ultimate boy's dream of a space rocket, orange and all; Gordon was the aquanaut in the mini-sub Thunderbird 4 and poor old John was stuck out in space orbit in Thunderbird 5, the monitoring station. Between John and Jeff, International Rescue could operate and communicate anywhere in the world or beyond.

While the sons were named after real astronauts Scott Carpenter, Virgil 'Gus' Grissom, John Glenn, Gordo Cooper and Alan Shepard, their looks were based on popular actors of the day. Scott was based on Sean Connery (check out the lips), Virgil allegedly either on James Garner or Roger Moore, John on Adam Faith and Charlton Heston, and Alan on Robert Reed. Jeff was based on Lorne Greene. Gordon never had a real model, though I never liked his glassy cross-eyed look anyway.

Along with the Tracy family were Jeff's mother, Kyrano their cook and all-round servant, and his daughter Tin-Tin, who was close to Alan. The main man behind the creations was the super-intelligent genius, Brains. International Rescue also employed various agents around the world, their best one being Jeff's old friend, Lady Penelope, based in her English countryside manor, with her butler/chauffeur/jack-of-all-trades, Parker. Her pink Rolls Royce, FAB1, was a gadget-laden, weapon-ready, monster on six wheels.

While International Rescue faced many trials and tribulations, difficult rescues, traps, hoaxes and adventures, their main enemy was a nameless man of Far Eastern appearance, later named 'The Hood'. He tried on several occasions to lure International Rescue into traps to steal their technology for other unknown forces. He was also the half-brother of Kyrano and had some form of psychic bond with him that he tried to exploit to no avail.

My favourite episode is 'The Uninvited' which contains a perplexing paradox. Scott had left Tokyo and was on his way back to base in the South Pacific, yet he was over the Sahara desert, when he was shot down by unfriendly aircraft. I have always wondered why he was over Egypt. Was he flying a decoy pattern to fool any tracking devices or surveillance or just patrolling? Anyway, the unfriendly bunch had a secret pyramid and were up to no good, so after being rescued by a couple of lost archaeologists and eventually by Virgil, they destroyed the pyramid. I also liked that the unfriendly bunch, the Zombites, spoke in a non-translated language, lending a more authentic and mysteriousness to being trapped in a foreign land.

My favourite part of any show was the full take-off preparation for Thunderbird 2 from Virgil's turn on the revolving wall panel to when Thunderbird 2 emerges from the reclining cliff face and the palm trees slump down. I still always love that split-second pause just before blast off and still swear that those big red engine booster pods will scrape against the launch pad ramp. Thunderbird 2 may look ungainly and a gaudy green, but in the sky, it is the best flying machine ever invented.

With the countdown introduction, stirring music and the well-known FAB catch-phrase (really just short for fabulous), the Thunderbirds had more fabulous machines and undertook the most inventive, dangerous and most epic of missions ever committed to screen. Even blockbusters today could not contemplate a skyscraper moving machine, a giant multi-legged army vehicle, a building-sized road builder or even a fashion show aboard a doomed supersonic jet.

Thunderbirds was great drama, even in supermarionation, the advanced puppetry techniques. Along with other popular Anderson productions, like Captain Scarlet and Stingray, it regularly pops up on British TV, entertaining new generations of Thunderbirds devotees.

08/May/2008

Entertainment – Movies (Other)
Testimonies: Why we love and hate going to the cinema

My Cinema-going Experiences

2020 visions
And just as I was getting used to splashing out on VIP seats along came the Covid-19 pandemic. It will be a whole new experience when/if I go back.

As it is, I wrote the above in July. In September, I ventured out for a double-bill at my local cinema, my first real social outing since the lockdown in London (March to July). While I was disappointed that more people didn't wear masks, the cinema did a good job with spacing and hygiene practices and I enjoyed my large salted popcorn mixed with a particular brand of multi-colored button-shaped chocolates. However, it will probably be next year before I venture out again.

There's nothing better than enjoying a great film on the big screen, so I love going to the cinema when I have the time and money. And even though I like going by myself, preferably to my local cinema, I know that I won't be alone in experiencing the film surrounded by other appreciative film-goers.

However, there are a few issues and experiences I like and despair of while trying to enjoy the films. First, I have saved up my time and money and picked the date and time to see my film, say Iron Man, rated 12A (under 12s admitted with Adult). Yet when I took my seat, surrounded by other young adults/adults, in walked a family with 2 small kids. The whole section I was in sagged with depression. Kids! It's 2100hrs –adult time. Why are the kids here? And in front of me! I envisioned them talking all the way through, not understanding it or asking mommy or daddy to go toilet or for food. I was silently fuming, especially when the dad got up during the film to get he kids booster seats since they couldn't see properly –ah, bless. But mercifully, the kids were quiet enough, a far cry from other experiences with kids in cinemas. But I still consider that after a certain time is adult time and that parents who do this are selfish and inconsiderate to us singletons, other child-free persons, and those who wanted to get away from their kids and have a child-free evening. So spend time with your kids during their time, not mine!

Double-headers. Americans are more used to this term than my fellow Brits and when I am strapped for time, but want to see a couple of films, I just see them on the same day back to back. The first time I did this was while I lived in New York and saw Batman and Star Trek V on the same night. I have since done that a couple of times maybe with a quick meal in between, but I satisfy my own inner film-going self. So far I have not attended any longer marathon film sessions, but maybe one day.

Sub-titles are a boon to films. I love watching Japanese and Chinese films with sub-titles. With dubbing you get silly voices and lose the nuances and music of the original voices. But sometimes sub-titling can be a curse. While in Lima, Peru, I watched Gladiator (for the fourth time) with some friends and the cinema was packed with adults and kids, but it was the incessant talking that got to me (that and the stickiest floors ever). Since the people didn't have to keenly watch the action or listen to the actors, they could just read the screen and talk to their friends at the same time. Very annoying, though none of the other Peruvians seem to mind.

I won't even go into mobile phones –just switch them off or if on silent/vibrate -don't answer it. You're at a film –you 'E-jit'.

My favourite film snack is salted popcorn and I sorely miss the hot butter that some Canadian and American cinemas served on top. British cinemas may be pricey, but they are trying to bring in as many luxuries with bar/lounges, alcohol, bigger range of food, better seats, and updated decors. It is debatable whether films are better or worse than before, but for me the thing I love is that the cinema is still alive and well, and I for one, despite some of my gripes above, will continue with my patronage of the big-screen, magical palace.

09/May/2008

Entertainment – Television (Other)
How can people spend so much time watching TV?

Watching TV – An Addict's View

2020 vision

Twelve years on and I'm still an addict, though my viewing habits have changed with better scheduled viewing hours and the recent streaming and binge-TV options at the forefront. I'm not one for watching series on my laptop as that takes away from writing time nor do I spend time watching on my phone while travelling as that takes up reading time. Gone are the talk shows and a lot of news, with sci-fi the bulk of my viewing pleasure. Let's just call that research for another project I'm working on.

I am a TV addict. I know I watch a lot of TV, but knowing that I do and that I do it for my own reasons makes my TV watching experience all the better.

As a single person I get the best out of my TV and make sure I watch what I want, when I want by circling what I really want to watch in red ink; a bit OCD, but then I don't end up watching anything I'm not interested in or any extraneous programmes. It doesn't always work, but by and large, self-restricting my TV hours works for me. I couldn't stand a TV being on just for background noise or to relieve boredom, that's just a waste of time and energy. I watch what I need to and want to, when I want, and nothing more.

I use TV as a portal for entertainment, learning and critical thinking. I love action adventure, sci-fi, epics, Westerns, documentaries, a smattering of reality shows and game shows, a couple of talk shows and the news. Not much surprises me, so genuine good TV with great plots is a relief or even a great sporting event. Finding that moment on TV that really surprises or inspires you is well worth the wait. TV is a tool, it broadens my world without dulling my mind or restricting my social life –though I have a video recorder just in case.

There is a lot to learn from TV. There are hundreds of documentaries and other programmes, of varying quality, according to personal choice, and some learning, especially in a subject you were not completely aware of, is better than nothing. There is a trend toward sameness, dumbing down, repeats, and creativity decline, but as with [the writing site], ratings take care of those weak and ineffectual programmes. People know what they like and TV execs respond to that, so next time you are watching TV, think about the type of person it was aimed at and why you are watching it.

TV makes me think. I like writing stories and my own proposals for TV programmes, and I watch TV to make sure I'm not rehashing familiar territory and that my ideas are generally original and sound compared to others. I like to anticipate story lines and imagine how I would do it. I have written a dozen or so synopses, sent a few off, but still have a lot to learn. So, let me get back to my TV watching and learn more from the TV master-scripters.

TV is also a starting point for my personal critique of the world. I watch and listen to news reports and talk shows, and form my own opinions instead of blindly believing all that is reported. I lean more to the right, but watch a few liberal news shows. It comes in handy when playing devil's advocate, especially in pub debates with friends. TV should make you think critically for yourself, make you do things for yourself, and make you feel outwards for others. TV should be a uniting medium, but the target audience has fallen under the spell of TV Svengalis, who have also forgotten and forsaken their remits, whether public or corporate. And that's when your own independent and discerning thoughts kick free and realise that you are in control of what you watch and think.

Is TV on the decline? Probably not, it's just reflecting our modern age, including society's failings. The media are not the trend-setters or the moral compass of society, but vice versa. TV, however, does have a huge influence upon our lives. A friend recently told me 'A dog has a master, but a cat has personnel.' Well, we are the pets of TV. It is our master and we are its personnel doing what the people in TV-land want us to do through compulsive viewing, advertising, branding, propaganda, grooming, and other means 24/7. So TV is not in decline, it's thriving away at our expense, because we let it do so.

I simultaneously feel sad, surprised, disappointment and admiration for those who don't own TVs. I do think that they are missing out and denying themselves an opportunity to experience that part of society. On the other hand, they're not outcasts and have chosen to disengage from a form of media no longer relevant to them. They're free from the dumbing down dilemma, free of TV schedules messing up any social life they might have, and free to read a book (the second generation TV, the first being the caveman's fire). But are they any different? Are they smarter, or dumber, prone to wearing glasses; are they computer geeks or pub crawlers? What do they substitute, if anything, for watching TV? Or is that a disingenuous, overly-suspicious remark, because they are not conforming to the perceived norms? Are they really better off without a TV?

So, yes, I am a TV addict, but I control my dosage. There is no cure for the TV drug, not even to those who abstain, since there are always second-hand effects and they are infected in some way. As with anything, take everything in moderation and that includes TV watching. Don't over-saturate your brain with TV, let it breathe and think for itself, learn and create, analyse and criticise, and you'll find that your TV watching experience will enhance your life.

11/May/2008

Entertainment
Celebrating the best creators of cult TV

Comparing the Legends of Cult TV

2020 vision
The list is still more or less intact, though Chris Carter was eventually rescued from the alien probes to resuscitate The X-Files, while Whedon and Abrahms graduated to the big screen.

Since the 1960s, each decade has seen the rise of a creator/writer of TV shows that have become cult viewing. Towering figures like Gene Roddenberry and Irwin Allen started the ball rolling, with Glen A. Larson and Stephen J. Cannell carrying the torch through the 1980s, and Josh Whedon and JJ Abrams taking up the challenge beyond the nineties. These fan-favourites are the Gods, legends and heroes of cult TV.

1960s and 1970s:
Irwin Allen was responsible for the emergence of over colour-saturated, inventive sci-fi series like Voyage to the Bottom of the Sea (1964), Lost In Space (1965), Time Tunnel (1966), and Land of the Giants, among others. He later became the 'The Master of Disaster' with films such as The Poseidon Adventure (1972) and The Towering Inferno (1974). Allen brought fun to implausible premises and a distinctive look in characters, costumes and a bright, B-movie quality to the sometimes ropey effects and plastic planets. Lost in Space and The Poseidon have had the modern-day remake treatment.

Gene Roddenberry rivalled Allen during the 60s and 70s until the Star Trek franchise took off, elevating the 'Great Bird of the Galaxy' into space, literally (with his ashes launched into space). Roddenberry started off with the non-sci-fi The Lieutenant' in 1963, leading up to Star Trek (1966) –which inspired a flurry of later series and films, with JJ Abrams directing the next in 2009. There then followed short-lived, but thoughtful TV films and series such as Genesis II (1973), Planet Earth (1974), and The Questor Tapes (1974). While various Star Trek series held court in the '90s, the Roddenberry inspired and revamped series like Earth: Final

Conflict (1997) and Andromeda (2000) showed why Roddenberry was a creative and introspective series creator/writer using sci-fi to illuminate deeper issues about mankind and its future.

A honourary member of this group is Gerry Anderson and his supermarionation and live-action creations like Fireball XL5 (1962), Captain Scarlet (1964), Stingray (1964), Thunderbirds (1965), Joe 90 (1968), UFO (1970), Space: 1999 (1975) and The Protectors (1972), which regularly pop up on British TV, entertaining new generations of Anderson devotees.

1980s:

Glen A. Larson brought a wide-ranging portfolio to the Cult TV table. Emerging from the late 70s with Battlestar Galactica (1978) and Buck Rogers in the 25th Century (1979), Larson then created two long-running classics with Magnum P.I. (1980 –with Donald P. Bellisario) and Knight Rider (1982) with The Fall Guy sandwiched in between. Other short-lived series were Automan (1983), Manimal (1983), and The Highwayman (1988). His series turned relative medium actors David Hasselhoff, Dirk Benedict and Tom Selleck into huge household names. While his series were entertaining, there was always an element of 'seen that, done that' in that a lot of footage or repeated sequences were borrowed from other films or series, especially in The Fall Guy and Buck Rogers. Nevertheless, Larson's legacy lives on in the new Battlestar Galactica series (2003) and an oft talked-about new Knight Rider project.

Stephen J. Cannell is the over-achiever to Larson's 'lazy' accomplishments. Also forging a reputation from the 1970s with series like The Rockford Files (1974), Baa Baa Black Sheep (1976), into the 80s with The Greatest American Hero (1980), The A-Team (1983), Hardcastle and McCormick (1983), Hunter (1984), Riptide (1984) and 21 Jump Street (1987) -which launched the career of Johnny Depp, and The Commish (1991), Cannell's work is also wide ranging and mostly set in real life situations. Law and order seems to be Larson's and Cannell's forte, but Cannell had a bit more panache, more character depth and certainly more longevity. Another similarity to Larson is that they concentrated on TV series during their heydays, though The A-Team is reputedly getting the movie screen makeover.

The successor of the 80s creators was Donald P. Bellisario earning his spurs under Glen A. Larson and Stephen J. Cannell, and creating Magnum, P.I. (1980 –with Glen A. Larson), Tales of the Gold Monkey (1982), Airwolf (1984), Quantum Leap (1989), JAG (1995), and is still going strong with NCIS (2003). Bellisario also ventured into the sci-fi market, though his main characters were usually of the ex/serving military ilk. Bellisario has distilled what made the 80s show popular and long-lived and ramped them up for his series for the nineties and noughties.

The Noughties whiz-kids

Joss Whedon burst onto our screens in 1997 with the TV series Buffy – The Vampire Slayer -revamped (pun intended) from the film flop- followed by Angel (1999) sealing his place in Cult TV fandom. But that was not enough and though the critically acclaimed Firefly (2002) series was short-lived, it spawned an even better movie version: Serenity (2005). Dollhouse is his newest offering, which has yet to air. Whedon also had a writing hand in Toy Story (1995), Titan A.E. (2000), and Alien: Resurrection (1997). He is also involved in writing comic books like X-Men, Fray and a continuing Buffy franchise. There are many strings to his bow, which makes it seem as if Whedon has disappeared, but while he does not crank out a huge cannon of work, it is certainly a volume of witty, sophisticated and pure guilty pleasure fare.

JJ Abrams, like Roddenberry and Bellisario before him, seems to be the eclipser of this particular generation of Cult TV creators. From Felicity (1998), to Alias (2001) –launching Jennifer Garner's career, Lost (2004), and two short-lived series The Catch (2005) and exec-produced Six Degrees (2006), Abrams has captured the action adventure/concept TV genre. Also a writer for films, Abrams started with Regarding Henry (1991), Forever Young (1992), and Armageddon (1998), before graduating to film directing in Mission: Impossible III (2006), Cloverfield (2008) and soon the newest Star Trek film (2009). Unlike the rest of the field, Abrams seems more capable of sustaining a movie directing career, though I hope to see him once more in charge of a small-screen gem.

Shining briefly in the nineties was Chris Carter, creator of The X-Files (1993), Millennium (1996), The Lone Gunmen (2001), and from who a couple of his stable writers graduated to create Space: Above and Beyond (1995). He has since disappeared. Alien abduction?

These then, are the giants, the legends, the Gods, which have shaped adventure and sci-fi cult TV over the last forty years. It is a select group, showing that genius and profligacy in creating and writing hit TV shows is rare and deserving of the eternal worship of their adoring fans.

16/Sep/2008

Entertainment – TV genres
Smallville: Ideas for future episodes

Super Ideas For the Future of Smallville

2020 vision
To be fair, most of my fellow writers in this title also wanted to introduce Batman and/or Wonder Woman to Smallville, which of course never happened in the series, nor yet in the CW Arrowverse. There have been hints and teases so let's see what 2021 brings...

So Smallville is winding down with core actors and production staff leaving the show. I think the writers had done quite well in weaving together a re-imagination of the Superman mythos and including the introduction of the emergent Justice League. Now they have to finish it off and introduce the two most important people in Superman's future life: Bruce Wayne/The Batman and Diana Prince/Wonder Woman. That is Superman's destiny, to form the 'Trinity' of the DC Universe that drives the Justice League. Even though Smallville is loosely based upon the comic book version, the TV writers have included a lot of the DC heroes and other peripheral figures, but not the Dark Knight and the Amazon Princess, so with that in mind, how to bring them in before the end?

Bruce Wayne:
Maybe the writers don't want to step on the toes of the new Batman franchise, but all Smallville needs to do is a one or two arc episode where Bruce Wayne comes to Metropolis for some gathering of the big-wigs, probably an auction of some valuable artefact, which secretly holds some power, and there are Ollie (Green Arrow) and Lex (guest staring) who check out the foppish new boy. They have a battle of wits and in the end Wayne wins the auction. But before he can leave Metropolis with his spoils, Wayne is kidnapped by unknown forces who steal the artefact (of course for Lex), but before Wayne is dispatched he is saved by Green Arrow. Wayne doesn't show that he's impressed, but as Green Arrow leaves and the (ever late) cops arrive, Wayne makes mental notes about costumes and weapons.

It just happens that Chloe is sent to report on the story and Clark tags along to get clues and info for Ollie. In his indifferent guise, Wayne seems arrogant and awkward, but Clark, having seeing this type of 'face' on Lex breaks through the barrier and befriends Wayne. It's here that Wayne realises that if he can trust anyone, it is Clark. But for now, he as his own mission to carry out.

Of course Wayne isn't the bumpkin he makes out to be and had put a tracker on the artefact. Turns out someone has been stealing related artefacts for sometime from Gotham and Wayne was investigating. We see him training in a gym, a proto-Batman. And as dark falls, a figure emerges from a back alley and heads for a warehouse on the docks. It's not The Batman as we know, but a man in a black-hooded, Kevlar-lined top with a mask and a modified army-issue webbing belt.

Ollie has his own mission. He had placed a tracker on one of the escaping kidnappers and he heads for the docks. Wayne is high up in the beams ready to pounce when Green Arrow rushes in, quickly deals with the half dozen bad guys and recovers the artefact. Wayne sees his chance and jumps Green Arrow and a fight ensues to a stalemate. Green Arrow asks who the mysterious man is and that he's returning the artefact to its rightful owner. Wayne realising he's telling the truth says he was there to do the same thing. A modicum of trust ensues, just as a car screeches outside and Clark and Chloe come running in. Arrow looks around to see that the man has disappeared.

After, as Wayne is given back the artefact, Clark drops by to say goodbye. They shake hands and Wayne leaves for Gotham. Chloe jokes that maybe with Lex and Ollie as billionaire adventurers, maybe Wayne is one too. Clark doubts it.

There is more interaction between Green Arrow and Bruce Wayne as Wayne will eventually become the financial clout behind the JLA, so some confrontation was needed to foreshadow this. So while they start out as friends, tensions will lead to their eventual falling out, somewhat like Clark and Lex.

Diana Prince:
In another episode, Clark finds himself stranded/lost in South America, somewhat amnesiac. He is befriended by a woman named Diana and they seem to be running from a beast who she says has killed all the villagers

around. There are all sorts of trials and tribulations in which they have to use their powers to escape and fight, but eventually the beast is caught. But should it be killed? Clark is given the option, but refuses, whereupon the beast turns into a child. It was a test and Clark has passed. He is also attracted to this mysterious woman. As he is about to kiss her. He falls unconscious, only to be awoken by Ollie and the Justice League who have been searching for him (in dispersed bits in the episode). Clark can't remember what happened, only that he had met a seemingly goddess of a woman.

The woman in question is back on her island and reports back to her mother, Queen Hippolyta that she is ready for her mission and that she has an ally she can count on. Her mother agrees and allows her daughter to enter Man's world on a quest of justice.

There was always a will they/won't they with Superman and Wonder Woman as they are 'ultimate' beings, so here begins their story.

So, whatever way Bruce and Diana are introduced, quick cameo/one episode appearances will set them up nicely to fulfill Clark's destiny without having to have over-blown entrances.

27/Sep/2008

Entertainment – TV Genres, Game Shows
TV show reviews: Deal or No Deal

The Appeal of Deal or No Deal

2020 Vision
Daytime TV – you gotta love it if you're unemployed – from breakfast news, The Wright Stuff, Loose Women, and daytime quiz shows. This is one of the many subject titles I introduced. I loved the simplicity of this game. But of course once back at work, I lost interest and haven't watched it since.

I love this show. The British version of Deal or No Deal always has me on the edge of my seat. It is such a random game with great host/contestant/audience interaction, fuelled by the bullish nature of the unseen Banker. It can bring you to clap and cheer for the big money win, shout at the TV screen for them to deal, or to stare in silence when someone's game absolutely collapses. But why does this simple game draw me in so much?

The success of this game show is in its unpredictability and the aforementioned interaction between the principal characters. With 22 boxes to open with values ranging from 1p to £250,000 by varying contestants with distinct personalities we get to know over time, there is that element of intimacy. The host, Noel Edmonds, a seasoned presenter knows how to relate to the contestant and audience, both in studio and at home, as well as how to egg on the Banker, who makes a monetary (or a swap or a gift package) offer after each box opening, often with dark, delicious, witty sarcasm. His invisible, yet omnipresent, character is a masterful stroke of creating suspense.

This is the contestants' show, more than any other game show, as they reveal their personalities and personal stories to the nation. For the more popular characters it's a chance to celebrate or commiserate in their triumph of 'spanking the Banker' or going home with nothing, maybe even 1p. Their reactions, their motivations, their greed and cautiousness are what make Deal or No Deal such compulsive viewing. It's great to see a contestant take a gamble and win big, though there are some where greed has taken over.

The £250,000 has only been won once by Laura ('She who must not be named' –according to The Banker), though the sum of money has come to the table or been left as one of the last two boxes on numerous occasions, but the contestant has already dealt or it is in a fellow contestant's box. There has been only one person who I would have begrudged winning anything. She was young, gorgeous, and blonde and might I say, without exaggeration, a total airhead; totally enamoured with the celebrity culture, yet she could not tell Noel what her company manufactured. Her reason for wanting to win big was that she felt she deserved more. Some contestants have had heart-breaking stories or difficulties in life, yet here was some ingénue barely out of her training bra and she felt she deserved more merely for the fact that she lived and breathed among us lesser mortals. I was so glad went she dealt early, missed out on another huge offer and then it was revealed that she did indeed have the £250,000. How she cried; and how I rejoiced -justice for once in a random game.

And that is the crux of the game. Some people loathe its supposed low brow approach; no questions, no skill; but that in itself is the beauty of Deal or No Deal. There is a strategy among the complete randomness of having picked the numbers. Some box numbers seem to either attract a blue (1p to £750.00) or a red (£1000.00 to £250,000) number or some players seem to do the same for many games. There is also the 'skill' in bluffing or manipulating the Banker into higher offers, especially if the power five (the top five red numbers) are still hanging around. The Banker respects decorum and appreciation for his offers and some contestants have found their flippancy rewarded with low offers. It is a game of chance, but you have to be ready to take that chance.

And that is the curse and pleasure of the so-called 'Dream Factory', knowing that divide between need and greed. Too often people in need are drawn into the game, often not wanting to disappoint their fellow contestants and the TV audience and then they die an awful death winning a lowly amount, whereas there have been a canny few who have dealt early, maybe regretting a later larger offer, but going out on a high. But that is the appeal of the show, it's a microcosm of the human condition, the choices we face every single day that will either enrich or lessen our lives. No matter how we phrase it or face it, life is that question: Deal Or No Deal.

29/Oct/2008

Entertainment - TV genres
Are the Daleks the most evil TV aliens created?

The Most Evil TV Villains

Are the Daleks the most evil TV aliens created? Well to assess this there has to be a multiversal war of epic proportions and I'm about to start it. I'm also going to cheat and include a few diabolical movie sci-fi movie villains, since the Daleks have featured in a couple of Doctor Who films and also because the other sci-fi films have been shown on TV. Below are the main categories of villains. I have not included comic book characters. This is a battle to the death and the results might surprise you.

I've split the super villains into 6 groups which I shall call Mech-organic, Machines, Massed Warriors, Superbeings, Creatures, and Other. They will war amongst themselves within and between groups. This could take some time, so sit back and enjoy.

Mech-organics:
First we'll start with the Mech-organics, which includes the Daleks, Cybermen, and Borg, because they contain some organic component within their mechanical exoskeletons or are technologically-enhanced beings.

Jumping straight in, the Daleks and the Cybermen fought each other to a standstill at Canary Wharf until The Doctor intervened, but I believe the Daleks would still have had the edge as they had aerial advantage and are master strategists. They probably would have found the Cybermens's weakness to gold (if it still is the case) or picked apart the Cybermen's vestigial base emotions.

The Borg Queen would probably be intrigued, but disgusted by the Daleks. She would covet their technology, but ultimately the bio component of the Borg would suffer against the Dalek weaponry. Plus Daleks would modulate their personal shields against Borg weapons and their exoskeleton would prevent any attempts to assimilate them or they would self-destruct. The Borg may prefer an alliance with the Cybermen, but while their agendas and ambitions are superficially the same to delete/convert or assimilate organics and technology, they would end up infighting. Here, the Collective mind of the Borg might have a slight advantage able to assimilate both Cybermen and their technology. Still, it is the Daleks that would win this group.

Machines:
This includes the Replicators (from Stargate), Terminators, Cylons (sorry –old style silver clunkies, as I have not seen the new one), and the Decepticons. These are wholly sentient, mechanical beings, some with synthetic skin to look human.

The battles between them would be exhaustive affairs with no clear winners, unless alliances were formed or another advantage developed. Apart from the Replicators, the rest are based upon humanoid foundations, which could be their weaknesses. The Replicators could possibly be the winners, spreading across the universe like nano-tech grey goo. They would be like annoying space spiders more deadly than the Bugs (from Starship Troopers). As seen, only time traps and super weapons would stop them so the Daleks, Borg, The Master, and Q may be the only ones who could defeat them.

The Decepticons would find it hard-going against the massed warriors (below) and other mechanical beings, as they are susceptible to projectile weapons. The Daleks would destroy them and the Borg would assimilate them to create Decepticon-drones. However, I believe that their intelligence would serve them well against the Terminators with their transforming abilities. Against the Replicators, the Decepticons would be eaten through and re-created as Repticons. Look out Optimus Prime!

Superbeings:
Here be the Goa'uld, Q, Sylar, The Master, Sith Lords and dark side Jedi, and The Devil (from Reaper).

The Goa'uld, though powerful and evil, can be held at bay or destroyed by humans so Daleks would make mince meat of them. Could a snake infect a Dalek to create a Goa'uldalek? Not likely. The Daleks most likely have an impenetrable anti-infiltration system as they can survive in the vacuum of space, a trait only seen in Replicators, Borg, Decepticons and possibly the Devil. The Goa'uld rule through massed warriors and slaves, so once they were defeated the Goa'uld would essentially be powerless.

Q is a non-corporeal being who manifests himself as a human. Q could possibly take out the Daleks and all the others, but we have not seen the source or full extent of his powers. The Daleks could also travel time and alternate dimensions to attack the Q Continuum. In a way, the Q are basically Time Lord types with powers, but could the ultimate mech-organic creation ever devised destroy the Q. The Borg would give it a good go against Q, though he has no technology per se. But Q's powers, though magic-like are still a higher form of science and the Borg would covet such a technological leap.

We know Q can be evil at times, but he is more impish and testing of others. The Devil however is evil, no matter how mercurial he acts. He would have fun in the battles, but his greatest problem would be that the Machines would have no soul to corrupt (except maybe the assimilated human Borg drones) and the others would be alien, so his powers may be ineffective against those who do not believe in him even if they are evil. Is the Devil the personification of all evil or just a human myth?

The evil Sith Lords and their dark side Jedi have considerable control over mechanical objects, but how would the Force fare against the Daleks? Could the Daleks resist Jedi mind tricks? I actually think that once the Daleks, Cybermen, and Borg figured out what the Force was (an emanation from all living things) they would nullify it, even if locally. The dark Jedi are not numerous or indestructible and a blast from whatever ray gun would surely kill them. There would be no second Empire.

The Master, as the antithesis of The Doctor; brilliant yet evil –has largely been forgotten behind the Daleks and Cybermen. He would be able to hold out for a while, but as the Daleks, Borg, and Terminators (to an extent) can travel time, he would be caught up in time wars of his own. The Borg could assimilate his Tardis and The Master would probably by taken prisoner by the Daleks and held like Davros or Baltar (by the Cylons), a traitor to his own. His hypnotic stare and Time Lord gadgetry would do him no good, though he could find the Borg's underlying 'software' weakness as Picard did and shut the Borg down. Terminator technology would be child's play to him, but the Daleks again would be his most potent foe. Or he could run into Sylar….

Sylar, though technically not an alien should still be considered because of his evilness. Even with his existing powers he could conceivably take out The Master or a Sith Lord. Able to travel time and have the use of the

Force, Sylar could be a match for the Daleks, though he could be imprisoned in a Dalek prison or a time lock. Sylar could be the only living thing to resist the Daleks. He'd have the knowledge and lives of a Time Lord, a TARDIS, the use of the Force and a lightsaber which could cut through Dalekian metal. Conceivably, with his ability to ascertain and fix how things work, could Sylar go for the ultimate prizes of the Borg Queen, a Dalek and even a Replicator, thereby controlling them? But what makes Sylar different from the Daleks is that what the Daleks do with a mechanical dispassion, Sylar would do with glee. Maybe that would be the Devil's evil influence.

Massed warriors:
Large fighting armies, warrior cultures and super troops include Stormtroopers, Sontarans, Klingons, Jem'Hadar, Wraith, and Predators. They are usually cloned and technologically enhanced. Also, apart from the Wraith, they are no evil per se, but minions of evil overlords or comprise of Empire structures. But even so, these shock troops would be cannon fodder to the groups above, basically due to their biological component being no match against superior technology and weapons.

The Predators may prove hardy, able to survive as supreme hunters, though we have not seen massed Predator fighting; they're mostly solitary hunters, but in breeding and hunting Aliens for sport, a whole army of Predators would despatch the rest easily, though the Sontarans would prove worthy adversaries. The Predators could also take on the Goa'uld, Sith Lords, Cybermen, Decepticons, Borg and Terminators. Q would prove too much and the Replicators would overwhelm them or maybe consider they would consider each other unworthy prey. But the Daleks again would be victorious due to seer numbers and superiority in tactics. The hunters would be out-hunted and exterminated.

Creatures:
This group consists of the Aliens, the Magog and the Spirit of the Abyss (from Andromeda), Bugs (Starship Troopers), vampires and werewolves. Being wholly organic would be a complete disadvantage. The only winner here would be the Aliens bred for their evilness, sheer ferocity, and acid blood. Against the mechanical groups, the Aliens blood may damage them, but repair systems and superior technology would destroy the Aliens.

The Magog and their mysterious creator, the Spirit of the Abyss, and their black hole weapons would be an unknown factor. A space battle at range may better suit them, though the Daleks, Sontarans, Cybermen, Cylons and Borg could possibility counter their weapons and once that was done the tooth and claw of a Magog would be no match for superior technology.

Vampires and werewolves? Not a chance, even if they did infect a few other beings, their weaknesses would be discovered. Even if all the massed warriors and creatures combined against the Machines, the Machines would win by exterminating, deleting or assimilating them.

Other:
Mr. Smith, the Matrix virus, is the lone representative here. Though the Smith virus was a product of a virtual reality, it could escape via a mechanical entity. He would devastate most of the Machines depending on their virus protection; Daleks, Borg, Cybermen, and the Replicators might survive the best, but as they share similar goals (at least to destroy humanity), Mr Smith could become an agent for any of them. But any alliance would not last as Mr Smith would view the Machines as decent batteries for a new virtual world. But viruses can be deleted, contained, or evolved to die off or co-opted for a new purpose so any control over reality would be limited.

Overall, the Daleks do seem to be the most powerful and evil. They are far more adaptable and able to span and conquer entire galaxies in time and space like no other evil being. In a battle against the Replicators, Dalek time technology would be to their advantage and against Sylar, they would no doubt build a prison to counter all his powers or shut down his brain, as death would be impossible (like an anti Capt. Jack from Torchwood). Sylar could be the last living organic being. But in future/alternate realities both the Daleks and Sylar are shown to be forces for good, so who knows how evil these creations are. Nevertheless, the Daleks do seem to have superiority over other evil characters and thus are Best in (evil) Show.

Those were some war scenarios, though there are a lot of ands, ifs or buts and contradictions. It would be interesting to know if there are any other worthy evil participants for the cross-universe war that could match the Daleks.

31/Oct/2008

Entertainment – TV genres
Finding the next actor to play Doctor Who

The Blacking up of Doctor Who?

2020 vision
I'm still ambivalent about iconic white characters being made over as black characters for no other reason than some white privilege guilt. Of course many of these characters were created by white men in times when black faces were rarely seen on screen or they were secondary characters. However, to say some of these characters need to be black to satisfy a new sensitive (black or white) audience or a politically-correct agenda would be wrong.

As a black writer of science fiction, most of my characters are white. I guess that's because I started reading and wanting to create comic books while I lived in Canada and most of the characters were white or aliens. I didn't set out to write a sci-fi novel series for or about black people, though some of my major characters are black. And as the world is changing what we need are more black creators creating their own universes, rather than transposing the current one. If people feel disenfranchised with what they see and hear then they should create their own worlds or their own industry like Nollywood and Afro-futurism. Personally, I don't feel I have to see a black character to empathise or identify with a character, TV show or film. In fact, I am currently watching many South Korean and Chinese programmes which instil such emotion in me unlike long-running favourite, though shallow, 'western' shows, that I identify with these characters more.

Since the article below was written there have been black Supermen, Wonder Women, and Batmen; a black Spider-man; and there's even a black female Doctor out there – brilliant! But they have all been their own individual identities rather than the original being black-faced.

Just having a person of colour take over from a white character is not enough in itself. If you are going to change a white character to a black character then that change would have to acknowledge and speak to their experience of being black, otherwise you may a well just black-face the character keeping the same script for the white actor. There has to be context. In fact, the show so far that has approached this beautifully is *The Watchmen* TV series (2019) who pulled it off in a powerful manner.

We humans are so creative. Surely we can find guilt-free ways to create original iconic black characters for the future that stand alone without having to erase the past.

So David Tennant will be stepping down as the tenth Doctor in 2010. Already there are a couple of front runners to replace him, the favourite being Paterson Joseph, a black actor. Don't get me wrong, Joseph is a decent actor; I've seen him in 'Jekyll' (against James Nesbitt – another favourite for the role), 'Green Wing', and 'Peep Show', but the character of Doctor Who is not that of a black man.

There is a tendency of the politically correct brigade to go overboard when re-casting long standing roles. The same was true of James Bond, when Colin Salmon was strong in the running, before the unfancied Daniel Craig made the role is own. Media chiefs in charge of such high-profile selections may argue that with The Doctor and James Bond, as long as the essence of the character is captured then whoever plays him should not matter, but I strongly disagree. Their creators envisaged their characters in a certain way, yes from being white men in a white-centred world of the 60s, but the two icons are now recognisable worldwide brands and to change due to any modern sensitivity to race is not the way to go. If it ain't broke, don't fix it, especially with gimmicks or a change for change sake.

If the powers-that-be want The Doctor to have a new experience then fine, but as a black Time Lord will there then be interspersed racial issues surreptitiously added, even though that was the role of various aliens and companions. The Doctor was the constant through these issues, like a law of the universe, and to break it on issues of equality would be wrong. I have nothing against black actors getting lead roles, especially as the hero, but leave the established characters alone.

I fear this is part of the Obamamania spreading around the world and people are leaping onto the bandwagon to exploit his ascendance: Change in America; Change in the TARDIS. The trend has started in supporting characters in film and comic books such as Felix Leiter in the Bond films, originally written and filmed as a white man, but his colour (and age) has changed over the years. The same is true for Nick Fury, leader of Marvel

Comic's SHIELD who had a colour makeover in the form of Samuel L. Jackson, who even supplied Fury's voice in 2008's Iron Man. Rather than create new and interesting black characters, the trend seems to be to 'black up' old characters to balance out the blanket whiteness that existed in recent years in British TV and film. But this could also serve to damage the appeal and spirit of certain beloved characters.

There has been no suggestion that Superman, Batman, Spider-Man, Harry Potter or Ms. Marple become black, why is that? Why tinker with an established character to please the pc crowd? Russell T. Davies is the wunderkind of the new revival of Doctor Who. He has even broke ground on sexuality and violence in Torchwood and dealing with young adult issues in The Sarah Jane Adventures, but if his successors are trying to be radical and modern in their assessment of Doctor Who, then a black Doctor would change the whole dynamic of the show and possibly alienate audiences.

There is a solution to this. This will be the 11th Doctor, who has a total of twelve regenerations (or thirteen lives) one of which could be the evil Valeyard if that was a valid reality. So after The Doctor finally sails off into the galactic sunset, why not reveal a hitherto unknown surviving city of Time Lords who take up the mantle of The Doctor and go forth on missions. The various Doctors could be white, black, female, or alien; a Time Lord version of the Green Lantern Corps or The Sons of Batman. If The Doctor were to be changed then where would it stop? After ratings that were out of this world, such a gambit could fail and cheapen the franchise which could see Doctor Who back in the doldrums as it was before its revival.

Who knows if there are rules governing Time Lord regenerations in regards to race and gender? As seen with the third Doctor it can even be imposed upon him. In previous inter-Doctor years, there was even talk of having a female Doctor, due to Romana's popularity, and who underwent an almost flippant voluntary regeneration. But I do hope that they leave Doctor Who's assumed ethnicity alone and let him be what he was created to be without gimmicks and hype to suit short-term objectives and racial agendas. So recast by all means, but be true to The Doctor and his fans.

08/Jan/2009

Entertainment – Movie Genres

Best Comic Book Films

2020 vision
Wow, what a difference a decade makes. Who would have thought the franchise juggernaut of the MCU would have dominated thereafter. For now, only the top two may make the list, with Marvel dominating over DC.

As a one-time avid reader of comic books, it's great to see some of them hit the big screen. There have been some great films adapted from Comic Books, but recently the bar has been raised as the right scripts, actors, director, and special effects have come together to realise all comic book readers' dreams. I have picked the five best films, in my opinion, that represent longevity in the comic book world and thus had more to lose than one-off Graphic Novels or shorter series. In descending order, these are:

5. Superman Returns (2006).
Brandon Routh, under the huge shadow of Christopher Reeves, hit the mark as the Returning Man of Steel. I was a bit disappointed with Director's Bryan Singer handling of the whole 'Son of Steel' bit, but maybe Jason will turn out to be a version of Connor Kent (Superboy) or end up in the future. Highlights included saving the airplane/shuttle and hoicking up the Kryptonite infested island. However, while Kevin Spacey did a good job of being Lex Luthor, Kate Bosworth was a disappointing Lois –not feisty enough. I hope the next film can veer away from Lex or Zod and introduce Darkseid, Brainiac or even Gog. Superman Returns was a soft reboot of Superman and while comparable to the first two original Superman films, it was still a little bit lacking in the legacy of Superman.

4. The X-Men franchise, with X2 (2003), being the best.
The first two were directed by Bryan Singer, while Brett Ratner directed X-Men: The Last Stand. Such luminaries staring were Hugh Jackman (Wolverine), Patrick Stewart (Prof. X), Ian McKellen (Magneto), and Halle

Berry (Storm). This film came out best because it dealt more with Wolverine's past, young mutants having to take sides, the attack on the mansion/Cerebro, and the precursor to Phoenix. It was evenly balanced and highlights included the brilliantly-realised opening scenes with Nightcrawler, Wolverine taking a shot to the head (ouch), and the slithering Mystique. X-Men 3: The Last Stand became livelier after Magneto took the Golden Gate Bridge for a stroll over to Alcatraz and cute little Ellen Page (Shadow Cat or Kitty Pryde) showed her moxy. While not all characters were completely sketched out or plots satisfactorily closed, the X-Men have been justifiably portrayed and long may it continue.

3. Spider-Man 2 (2004).
Directed by Sam Raimi, Tobey Maguire returns as the Webcrawler, while fang-toothed Kirsten Dunst makes the perfect Mary Jane Watson. The first film was an amazing introduction, but the third was too crowded even though Sandman and Venom were great characters. Out of the Spidey franchise, the second film epitomised the Spider-Man/Peter Parker synthesis of the hero. Not only did he have to constantly battle his inner doubts and demons, but also James Franco as the son of The Green Goblin and Alfred Molina's Doc Ock/Dr. Otto Octavius. Highlights include Spidey's swinging around New York delivering pizza and saving kids, the fantastic fight scene on the train, holding up the warehouse wall, and Mary Jane running away in her wedding dress (brought a lump to my throat). Unlike Batman, Peter Parker is a fallible hero, a human in a costume, which endears him to his fans (both real and fictional).

2. Batman: The Dark Knight (2008).
Christian Bale is the Gotham Knight here again, carrying on from Batman Begins, both Directed by Christopher Nolan. The production had matured all round and of course the late Heath Ledger as The Joker was the show stealer. Aaron Eckhart as Harvey Dent/Two-Face, Michael Caine as dependable Alfred, Gary Oldman as James Gordon, Morgan Freeman as the wily Lucius Fox, and Maggie Gyllenhaal as Rachel Dawes rounded out the cast, lending more credibility than all of the previous Batman films. Highlights included all scenes with the Tumbler/Batmobile and Batpod (I want one), the capture of The Scarecrow, the darkness of the Joker's mind games - especially on the ferries, and the 'trip' to Hong Kong. This incarnation of Batman works, because the makers have realised that Batman is the real character and that Bruce Wayne is the

mask. Batman is dark and obsessive about crime. As with Superman, however, instead of re-hashing old foes, they'll also have to introduce other Batman villains like The Ventriloquist, Clayface, Killer Croc, Man-Bat, and the real Bane.

1. Iron Man (2008).
Directed by Jon Favreau, Robert Downey Jr. as billionaire industrialist Tony Stark puts in one of his best performances. Gwyneth Paltrow suitably impressed as Pepper Potts, Terrence Howard was a perfect James Rhodes and a bald Jeff Bridges was the baddie Obadiah Stane. This is my favourite comic book film for a long time, though I really only know Iron Man from The Avengers. And while Batman is psychologically themed, Iron Man targets the political/industrial-military sphere, both quite relevant for our times. Highlights included building the first armour in the cave, learning how to fly, the confrontation with the F-22 Raptors, and the battle with Stane's Iron Monger. The slickness of the production, the Iron Man suit, and the sheer fun the actors are having really elevated Iron Man above the lacklustre series of the Hulk, Daredevil and Fantastic Four films. Out of all the Comic Book 'origin' films, Iron Man just hit all the right marks without a turgid love story or over-long back story. Iron Man was free of the baggage and hype other 'big' franchises brought with them. Iron Man just won out over Batman, because of the 'wow' factor and getting the technology and effects right for the armour, both inside and outside. Admittedly, I missed the post-credit scene, but are The Avengers far behind?

Bonuses: Hancock (2008). While not a comic book, Hancock's superhero actions are as infamous as the anti-hero Guy Gardner (Green Lantern) and should earn him some kudos in this title. Wanted (2008) was based loosely on a Top Cow graphic novel written by Mark Millar. But this fun, kick-butt action flick had Angelina Jolie in it, so what more could you want.

The big comic book films to watch out for this year are: The Watchmen (created by writer Alan Moore (1986) and Marvel's X-Men Origins: Wolverine. Maybe DC will finally challenge Marvel in the superhero stakes and release one of the best comic book films ever.

28/Feb/2009

Entertainment – TV Genres
TV show reviews: The Wright Stuff

The Wright Stuff

2020 vision
Another daytime show I would watch right after the morning news, which featured varied topics for discussion with celebrity and audience voices on the issues of the day. It was perfect for when I was unemployed and even furnished several ideas for essays in this book. It's still going now, but with a new host and show title, but I haven't watched it in years.

The Wright Stuff is a British talk show, hosted by former newspaper journalist Matthew Wright. The programme has been the cornerstone of (channel) Five's morning for the past ten years. It's a great blend of live chat, phone-ins, guest panels, and current issues discussions. There is plenty of audience interaction and occasional vox pop action from the streets.

Over the ninety minutes, Matthew introduces a regular guest panel, two of whom are usually around for a week with a third member being a guest for the day. This is one reason I like the show; it gives people a chance to see and hear a favoured celebrity speak their mind, instead of just reading lines or plugging a new book or film. They think for themselves. A few have disappointed as they have to spend time reading about the current issues of the day in newspapers and express their views. Some are better than others, while some seem to have no life beyond their chosen occupation. Others have surprised me in that before I thought of them as just a bimbo/himbo, but they are quite intelligent. It just goes to show that their on-screen character or media portrayal is quite often at odds with the reality. Panel members can include journalists, politicians, actors, doctors, other presenters, and comedians providing a good mix of professions and views.

After introducing and chatting to the one-day celebrity on the panel, the 'What's in the papers' session kicks off the show focusing on the stories of the day, which the guests read out and comment on. Then Matthew gets into the topics of the day. Off to one side of the panel desk is a young woman (currently Amie) in a booth who takes calls throughout the show, introduces them to Matthew, and often reads out e-mails and text messages. There is also a male member of the show (currently Eric) who sits in the audience and asks their opinion on topics.

The show usually has three debate points and a specialist section at the end, each section punctuated by ad breaks, which may feature a trivia question concerning the upcoming topic. The first debate of the show is usually a topical news subject, fresh from the papers and usually serious or controversial. The second part is normally a fun topic, for laughs and is a shorter section. The final debate topic is usually a social issue, sometimes funny, other times dramatic, which could cause or be the result of another topic from the week. The last section is an advice section where a professional discusses whatever issue is featured, taking calls from viewers. Whether about sex, relationships, embarrassing illnesses, colour schemes for life, healthy food, pets, or dreams; you name it, they'll discuss it. At the end of the show as the credits roll, 'booth girl' or 'audience guy' describe how you can get in touch with the show or be in the audience, to 'get yourself on the telly!'

Controversy has stalked the show as a live show is prone to. In 2002, Matthew accidentally named a celebrity as a rapist, which other news outlets had refrained from. Also, in 2005, when Prime Minister Blair was on the show, he was harangued by a woman who approached the desk asking about school issues. Recently, in February 2009, Matthew defended Carol Thatcher, a frequent panel member, who had made a racist remark (in private) on a BBC show from which she was fired. Finally, Matthew has also publicly displayed his dislike for bargain-basement daytime talk show host, Jeremy Kyle, who Matthew often gets mistaken for.

All in all, the show has everything you want for news, gossip, opinions, and celebrities. It has it pulse on the issues that matter to people. It is an alternative news show that reflects the public's views. It is issue driven; not celebrity-driven, but it shows the celebrities in a real light as real people with much the same problems and issues 'normal' people have. It allows celebrities to let their hair down and talk to and empathise with others, which actually enhances their appeal. The Wright Stuff definitely has all the right stuff.

27/Mar/2009

Entertainment – movie genres
Best western movies of all time

The Best Westerns

2020 vision
Still my favourites list. Most of the 'modern' revisionist Westerns would not make it; they try too hard and the authenticity of these recent stories, characters, and acting has sadly disappeared.

Over the years, I have watched countless westerns and have a list of over 150 that I like and probably more not on that list. There is just something about the Western that captures the imagination; the lifestyle and character of the cowboy, the lawlessness that had to be tamed, revenge and redemption, the horsemanship, the scenery, the plucky dames, and the inevitable duel. Out of all of those hundreds of films, I found the ten that most appealed to me.

10. The Magnificent Seven (1960).
On its own, this film is a classic and I still enjoy it. The tale of the Seven coming together and standing against insurmountable odds is a common theme, but this still is the best. However, I do prefer the much superior original 'The Seven Samurai' (1954). The only sequel that I like to watch is Guns of the Magnificent Seven (1969). Here George Kennedy takes over from Yul Brenner and Lee Van Cleef, and though the cast is inferior to the preceding classics, it is the ending that still floors me, as an anguished Kennedy looks around in despair at all his dead men in the Mexican fortress. All that death and destruction to free one man, even though that one man could free his nation. There are many tragic deaths in Westerns, but this is a finer poignant moment not often seen in Westerns.

9. Silverado (1985).
A young Kevin Costner steals the show as the cocky cowboy to his older brother Scott Glenn's more mature and reformed jailbird, who along with Kevin Kline's gunslinger, and Danny Glover's farmer eventually team up against bad Sheriff Brian Dennehy's gang. One of the better and original westerns of this decade that kept the west alive.

8. High Plains Drifter (1973).
Apparently, John Wayne walked out from the film on its premier because he thought it too violent. Clint Eastwood emerges from the shadows of the man with no name, to play, er, a man with no name. Clint has come to take revenge on a town and some marauding cowboy killers in retaliation for the death of a Marshall. As he rides into the sunset, you wonder if he's the Marshall's dead spirit, his son, or just a wandering guardian of justice of good deeds. Clint's gauntlet of bloodletting, fire, rape, red paint, and death may have been a wee bit over the top, but he got the job done.

7. The Wild Bunch (1969).
William Holden, Ernest Borgnine, Ben Johnson and Warren Oates reminded me of a Western A-Team gone bad. They're on a mission and on the run from their former member turned bounty hunter, Robert Ryan. Unfortunately, by the climax of Sam Peckinpah's film, with the best one-take sequence in Western history, the four turn against the Mexican revolutionaries and German soldiers and pay the ultimate price. They were four old cowboys on the cusp of a new age and they knew their time was up. But what a way to go! 'Pike, Pike!!'

6. Tombstone (1993).
Out of all the OK Corral gunfights, this one is the best, whether the story is accurate or not. The Earps were like pieces of windswept black granite holding the law, while the Clantons and the Cowboys tried to chip away at the bedrock of lawful society. Kurt Russell, as Wyatt Earp, held the film together as a moustachioed force of nature, while Val Kilmer was his sidekick Doc 'I'll be your huckleberry' Holliday. While the characterisation was great, the humour came out naturally as in the gun/tin cup 'duel' between Doc Holliday and Johnny Ringo (Michael Biehn) which was a fantastic touch. For a modern, slick, action-packed western, Tombstone was very emotional and atmospheric.

5. Dodge City (1939).
Errol Flynn in his big hat tilted jauntily to match his low slung belt sets an early standard for western with its humour and gunplay. It's the old tale of taming the west in order for the railroad and honest men to make a living. It also still has the best saloon fight, bar none, and I love the table flying in from the stairs. Throw in Robin Hood stalwarts Alan Hale and Olivia De Havilland, along with Guinn 'Big Boy' Williams and you have an absolute Technicolor classic.

4. Shane (1953).
Alan Ladd, may have been short in stature, but he towers in this classic western that sets trends in having jangling spurs and the gun twirl. Van Heflin, Jean Arthur and Brandon De Wilde are the homestead family to be saved, while Jack Palance makes an early sneering appearance as the villainous gunslinger out for Shane's blood.

3. The Good, The Bad, and The Ugly (1966).
Clint Eastwood (Blondie), Lee Van Cleef (Angel Eyes), and Eli Wallach (Tuco) star in this Sergio Leone classic Spaghetti Western. Even though his epic has great actors and action, it also has great music, a trait shared by my top three. The music, for each character, sublimely scored by Ennio Morricone, sets the scene and brings more presence to the film. Even now, people always remember the opening 'Waaaa' music. The word 'frenemy' could have been invented for the three protagonists as they vied and allied with each other to discover the whereabouts of the gold at the end of the frantic climax in the cemetery. While this is a violent film, the playful, glint-in-the-eye humour is there throughout, assuring the viewer that the actors are having as much fun as we are. This caps Clint's 'Man with no name' Spaghetti trilogy, cementing his place in the history of Western.

2. Once Upon a Time in the West (1969).
A convoluted tale of revenge, land ownership, and relationships, linked together by character-themed music. Leone and Morricone teamed up once more to produce another Western masterpiece. Charles Bronson's 'Harmonica', in name and sound, haunt the screen while hunting Henry Fonda's 'Frank', in name and demeanour ('Easy, Frank, easy'). Fonda is mesmerising as the bad guy, his cold, steely, blue eyes commanding the screen as soon as he and his gang step out from the dust, one by one, after slaughtering the McBain family. Claudia Cardinale, the McBain widow, is left to decide between Frank, Harmonica, and fugitive bandit Cheyenne (Jason Robards), as she comes into possession of valuable railroad land. This is a western of many levels, though I usually avoid the subtexts and enjoy the final duel of music and motion as we finally find out why Harmonica and Frank were destined to meet on a winding road of death. It hardly gets better than this.

1. The Big Country (1958).

I admit that my top three do change places every so often and holding top place now is this William Wyler epic. Gregory Peck (Jim McKay), Charlton Heston (Steve Leech), Burl Ives (Rufus Hannassey), Jean Simmons (Julie Maragon), Charles Bickford (Maj. Henry Terrill), Carroll Baker (Pat Terrill), and Chuck Connors (Buck Hannassey) head up the all-star cast in this family feud over land, water and women. Also, from the opening welcoming scenes of Jim McKay to the final rifle duel, the music of Jerome Moross powers the action, notably as the Major and his men race in Blanco Canyon the first time and in my favourite scene when the Major sets of alone like Napoleon down the canyon for the final duel reluctantly followed by a repentant Leech and then the rest of the hired hands. This is like a Western version of the Charge of the Light Brigade highlighting the blind loyalty and family ties that energise the film throughout. The Big Country is a study in character, writ large. It is about love, honour, and integrity, though each character has their own version of what these should be. The Big Country: a Western at its best.

27/May/2009

Entertainment – TV genres
Do TV police dramas affect the way real police and criminals operate?

Have TV Police Affected the Way Police and Criminals Behave?

The proliferation of cops and robbers shows, their depiction of the ingenious ways to commit and solve crimes, and the eccentricities of law makers and law breakers must in some way impinge upon the real world. But which drives which? Does fact derive from fiction or does fiction reflect fact? It is probably a bit of both, with real life providing the background/template for fictional action, but how much can a TV show influence what happens in real crime fighting?

Tactics:
While police tactics have evolved over the years to meet criminal trends and vice versa, how many have been affected by TV shows? Are there any statistics that reveal TV copy-cat crimes? Does a policeman say he saw something on TV and used it to solve a crime? Likewise, many TV shows sail close to the wind when writing episodes that match real-life cases, showing police tactics, specialist equipment, and inventive criminal methods and weapons. When fictional crime 'inspires' reality, do both the police and criminals take note of particular situations, even though the fictionalised account will be somewhat over the top?

One example is that ubiquitous device that can cut perfect circles in glass, after which the criminal then removes the glass. That device is fiction; glass does not cut like that. Another is the procurement, use, and alterations of high-powered weapons. Given their dominance and presumed effectiveness in TV shows, criminals are more than likely to imitate this, giving the police more problems. While U.S. police are routinely armed, they are not in the U.K. and debates as to whether British police should be armed occurs after each gun crime. This is one reason why some people in the U.K. call for violent (U.S.) shows to be screened later, censored, or rejected. But British police have responded and can now be armed with tasers. Whether knife, gun, and gang crime has been affected by violent police TV shows, it has had a dramatic effect on British police tactics.

Behaviour and habits:
With the increase of profiling, specialist units, and operational tactics shows on the TV, the criminal has an opportunity to study their methods and techniques. Not that it always works. The amount of ways to murder, harm, rob, kidnap, commit fraud, etc is endless, but in the end the criminal usually gets caught. The "sons of Columbo": 'Monk', the 'Mentalist', and 'Psych' are especially adept at reading people and solving crimes. The show 'Criminal Minds' takes us into the said mind of a criminal dissecting their motivations. Can someone watching and learning from these shows change their behaviour and habits in order to commit a crime scot-free or even impersonate law officials? Is there such a thing as a perfect crime these days? Can lie-detector tests be deceived? Are guilty people as transparent as made out on TV? Profilers have to stay one step ahead of the master manipulators.

There are countless TV shows with psychologists revealing tell-tale behavioural signs and real life 'mentalist' Derren Brown performing his own brand of cold-reading tricks and other feats of psychological 'magic'. Shows like the fictional 'Hustle' and scam-busting 'The Real Hustle' also reveal how behavioural techniques can be used as a tool toward crime. The human is the sum of inherited and learned attributes, knowing right from wrong, and how to use those experiences. If such psychological issues on TV shows are affecting viewers' habits and morality then the police have to step up their efforts to combat this, which then gets shown on TV, which affects people, etc. It's a never-ending battle to manipulate, anticipate, and control criminal actions and minds, but for how much longer can it continue?

Forensics and technology:
Though the forensics on the 'CSI' franchise shows are somewhat flashy and speedy, does the criminal have an advantage in knowing what they can do to escape detection, what is admissible in court, and how to corrupt evidence? Are there statistics on unsolved files for lack of forensic evidence, possibly due to smart criminals covering their tracks, learned from TV shows? When TV's 'Columbo', Peter Falk, read about a criminal being caught because of the imprint of his tooth on a piece of cheese, he used that in a memorable episode. People in courts expect flashy lawyers, conclusive forensics, and stereotypical villains in the dock.

What the people see on TV cannot be replicated in real life, so does trust of the system wane or are people aware of these discrepancies when on jury duty? CCTV and other surveillance devices; bugs, wires, and tracking gadgets; computers and mobile phones, etc, are all part of modern policing. So are counter-surveillance methods and techniques, seen in all good spy films. How many criminals are still free and undetected, because they carefully control their communication networks and public affiliations? How many hackers, crackers, and tech-savvy surfers contravene guarded firewalls spreading viruses or stealing information? Technology (so far) is only as smart as the people that built them and forensics only as infallible as the person investigating. Some police dramas make these two seem like the end all and be all, but they are not. They are just tools, made and used by humans, and as such can be disrupted and contaminated by people.

Media:
The longer a criminal stays free, the more publicity they get and like a police show, they start earning a name for themselves: 'The Strangler', 'The Beltway Sniper', 'The Moors Murderer', etc. Such elevation from anonymity must be a goal of criminals, to be a name, rather than a generic serial killer, gang leader, or thief. Almost all TV shows have some sort of nemesis with a colourful nom-de-plume, usually concocted by some media wag out to make a name for themselves. Sometimes, the real media picks up on things before the police, or at least publicises it more. But what can the police do? Should the media be used or blacked-out in order to protect case details and victims/witnesses? Of course, all police forces would refuse/deny using TV police shows to pick up tips, as they should do, but the more that TV police shows become more realistic they gain police cooperation and consultants. While the police units won't have special departments with officers that comb through TV police archives for similar crimes, does it get mentioned that such and such a show had a case similar that might be worth looking into? Shouldn't everything be done to solve the crime, including sourcing solutions from the TV cops? But how far is too far?

Mediums and psychics:
Many shows now feature psychics, with the fictional Allison DuBois (played by Patricia Arquette) from 'Medium' taking on the mantle of the real psychic Allison DuBois, who prefers to call herself a medium or profiler. Apart from this show, most other TV cop shows depict psychics

as frauds or incredibly lucky, but psychics are still used and advertise for business. The apparent success of the real Allison DuBois spawned a show about her. And while it may be reality that drove that, the publicity from it gives the real Allison DuBois and other psychics more credibility and added work. Such work could damage a police unit's reputation, thus lower its estimation in the eyes of the public.

The public and law:
Lastly, what about the general public? Crime is a media event, with some unlawful acts caught on mobile phone cameras or called into a televised crime show. Watching police dramas or documentaries with re-creations of crimes could help the public to identify a crime in progress, to avoid a dangerous criminal/situation, to report crimes, to be generally vigilant, or even have a criminal caught. Are people's views and expectations of law enforcement changing? Sneaky lawyers and criminals protesting their human rights also creeps between reality and TV.

People have little faith in the law, when reading or viewing such stories, thus police dramas featuring vigilantes and a serial-killing forensics officer in 'Dexter' have the public rooting for them. The public expects the police to do better in investigating and solving crimes. The TV police do it time after time in nice, neat packages. If only real life was that simple. How can real police compete against perceptions from TV cops? Well, all they can do is to keep their heads held high, get on with the job, and rely on us, the public, and their respective governments to give them the tools and respect needed for the job. While watching police dramas won't necessarily be a part of their academy training, the police will affect how TV portrays them to the public.

Police and crime shows may be helping crime pay for some, but the police are probably still one step ahead. There's too much violence on the streets for the police to be watching TV for ways to solving/monitoring it. But sometimes truth is stranger than fiction and somewhere out there are the next generation of law enforcers and criminals being inspired by what they see on TV. It's left to the future to see how those TV police shows and the real police respond.

25/July/2009

Entertainment
How society is reflected in comic books

Our Comic Book Society

Society often finds itself reflected in comic books, as comic books are the updated forms of our ancient forebear's myths and orals tales, which often reflected their society. Modern comic books, especially the superhero genre, found their genesis and popularity rise during the Great Depression years and WWII, the heroes reflecting a demoralised and war-torn societies' need for justice and morale-boosting victory.

Superheroes are heirs to the ancient gods, many of whom (e.g. Thor, Ares, and Hercules) now do appear in comic books. Society is not ready to give up on our ancient heritage of story telling of derring-do by people superior to ourselves. This is reflected in comic books by the support most of the heroes and masked vigilantes receive. Both real and fictional societies look up to and revere heroes for their deeds.

Mutants, of course, are the biggest reflections of our society within comic books. When Marvel conceived their 1960s icons, mutants represented the disaffected and misunderstood teenagers, the minority cultures or outsiders, which nowadays would include homosexuals and alternative cultures. Comic books can take these alternative cultures and craft unique characters with characters such as Northstar, Midnighter and Apollo being prominent gay superheroes. There has also been a reflection, possibly from Civil Rights advances and the Obama-effect as black heroes become more front-and-centre, especially with the transformation of Colonel Nick Fury from a major white character into the Samuel L. Jackson-inspired incarnation. As comic books have branched out over the world, more and more superheroes now come from all over the world, but those countries can now claim some superheroes as their own as major companies have allowed their characters to become ethnic variations, such as the Indian Spider-Man. Society has allowed comic books to go multi-cultural.

Our society often feels powerless against the increasing and random crime that occurs. With no extra police available, some parts of society feel that vigilantism is an acceptable form of self-defence and protective action.

Vigilantism is our fantasy; our dream of revenge and justice, which only the comic book societies can actively perform to their fullest and deadly outcome. We see our justice authorities as under performing, too lenient, or unable to cope, so the comic book heroes symbolise our ideal justice systems. However, in the comic books emergency services play second fiddle to superheroes and pick up the pieces, while our police, firemen, and medical crews have to achieve their super-heroic acts without the help from super-powered beings. While comic book services are overwhelmed by super villains destroying cities our services are under threat from funding cuts, bureaucracy, and low morale.

The DC universe often has their superheroes taking care of galactic issues, global crises, or super-criminal aggression, leaving us mere mortals to fend for ourselves. Superheroes do not rule the world. They see this as humanity having self-determination. Comic Book societies do not vote for their superheroes (excepting Oliver Queen/Green Arrow as Mayor of Star City and Tony Stark/Iron Man appointed as Secretary of Defence), and have no control over their operating procedures. As Globalisation, trans-nationalism, quangos, and unelected officials rule over our lives, often without the express permission of the voter, our self-determination is undermined. Corporatism has taken over, much like Lex Luthor and the Kingpin controlling their vast military-industrial complexes. Yet we have no superheroes to save us from nefarious schemes dreamed up by our politicians and businessmen. Our society cannot change from the current global system in place, despite climate change, economic meltdown, and terrorism telling us that we must change. Likewise, in the comic book societies they have superheroes who also seek to keep the status quo and let us little people fend for ourselves, until the next galactic invasion arrives.

Lastly, the media in our society have countless reports just on our celebrity and infamous cultures. This includes the naming and unveiling of serial killers, vigilantes, stalkers, and gang lords. In the 1990s in New York, Dart Man and the Zodiac Killer were infamous villains and recently the Unabomber was captured. Our society is still based around the campfire listening to stories of heroes and villains, except it is now on TV and the Internet 24/7. Media in the comic books is now reflecting society with some comics having panels with newscasters reporting on world events involving superheroes. Comic books have realised that the media, as well as lauding superheroes can also bring them down. In some ways, our celebrity culture mirrors the superhero culture in the comic books, though while our society would hound superheroes for their stories and secret identities, the comic books (until recently) seemed to leave superheroes alone. Superheroes now have to be more accountable for their actions.

Our society reflects quite often in comic books as our society changes. The violence, graphic story lines, and darkness of comic book characters have been on the increase as we find our society fractured, under threat from outside, and looking for new heroes. Our imagination of what our society needs are reflected within comic books, but it is not as straight forwarded as having Superman fly down to save us. We need to become heroes ourselves, to step forth and be the beacon of light, and for once let the comic books reflect upon our society.

16/Oct/2010

Entertainment
Reasons why some shows are better to watch on DVD than live on TV

DVDs Over TV

2020 vision
Oh, the days before streaming! When Netflix and Amazon started their online products, I hated the fact they short-changed us with series lasting only 8, 10, 12 or 18 episodes. What the hell was that about, I wondered? But now I see the value in high quality, focussed and streamlined shows without the padding. While I still have many a DVD collection for my most favourite shows, their downfall is that you have to wait several months after the TV viewing before the latest DVD is out. And even with having to pay for streaming, I now favour the online platforms. Though now I am spoiled, as I want to binge watch the whole series at once rather than even wait a week for a new episode! Not good for a TV addict.

There are many advantages to watching some shows on DVD over shows live on TV. This is especially true for the avid TV viewer who cannot always get to see their favourite shows for a myriad of reasons. In today's media-driven world, the competition for the viewer is relentless and the viewer has to make a choice as to what warrants his/her viewing attention over what is not worth viewing. DVDs offer the perfect choice in bypassing TV and watching what you want, when you want.

Convenience:
Shows on DVD offer the viewer the convenience of watching their favourite show in their own time and place. You don't have to wait for the following week for the next thrilling episode and everything is at your own pace, especially if there is nothing else on TV. Being portable, DVDs can be watched on a laptop or portable player at home or work or on the move. And of course, DVDs are strike-busters keeping the entertainment going while TV studios go on strike.

Extra features:
DVDs offer extra features like behind-the-scenes documentaries, cast and crew interviews, bloopers, and commentaries on the show. This is value-for-money in-house entertainment not often shown on TV. You can experience those special moments over and over and without commercials. Take the shows Lost or Heroes; the extra features enhance your viewing pleasure as it can fill in off-screen stories, explain plotlines, and explore the special effects in detail. Shows on live TV can never be the media platform that the DVD is.

Loyal viewing:
The effect of owning a DVD of a show will more likely bond the viewer to the show more so than the same show live on TV will. This creates a loyal following to the show. In the UK, some US shows are not shown on terrestrial TV, are edited for violence, or some shows are picked up for vast sums of money by satellite channels from terrestrial channels (e.g. Lost, Stargate, Medium, and Alias, etc), which makes it hard for the viewer to follow if they do not have satellite or cable. DVDs offer the ideal opportunity to loyally watch these shows without worrying which channel and time they'll be on next season, if at all.

International viewers:
Internationally, DVDs offer the English-speaking viewer the chance to listen to the original voices in English or have sub-titles, rather than watch badly dubbed versions. A show like True Blood is not currently shown in Germany, so DVDs present German viewers with the ability to see shows they would never get a chance to see otherwise. DVDs can transcend borders which TV cannot.

Future preservation:
A DVD box set offers future viewing prospects, with a whole back catalogue of shows to see. DVDs offer the chance for cult classics (e.g. Firefly, Lexx, or Fawlty Towers) to survive and be beloved by future generations, while old TV shows not on DVD have sunk without a trace. TV repeats of some shows are few and far between and the quality of the show's film over time will degrade, but DVDs offer a crisper digital picture for longer. And while DVD's offer the freedom of viewing shows at a price, the costs could be redeemed somewhat by reselling them to another fan of the show.

The digital versatile disc is certainly a flexible option over shows live on TV. The experience of watching your favourite show is much more palpable with the DVD, the viewer feeling he/she owns part of the show, while watching shows live on TV are fleeting hours of fading memories. Watching shows live on TV may have its benefits, but DVD viewing will always be a more meaningful event, lasting long after the show on TV has ended.

18/Nov/2010

Entertainment

British-owned Channel 4 network doesn't understand its viewers

Channel 4 and US TV programmes

2020 vision

This has continued with most of its US sci-fi products shifted 'off-world' to E4 (formerly T4), except for comedies which run ad infinitum. Channel 4 may then show repeats early Saturday mornings or late evenings. The channel may have its remit and responsibility to the audience, but then it has to deliver on its service and either commit to a show or not show it at all.

What is it with Channel 4 and the ever-shifting schedules of its imported US drama and Sci-Fi TV programmes? Only this week, *Smallville* returned for its 9th and penultimate season. While this super series was previously broadcast on Saturdays or Sundays in first runs on T4, it has now been relegated to weekdays at 11am, as if anyone will be around to watch it then. Instead of months for the show to play out and be savoured, *Smallville* will be run out in breakneck speed within a month, like a cheap repeat. That's no way to treat a popular first-run show. If it was half-term for kids or if it had been promoted it may have made sense, but no, nothing. Channel 4 has a history of treating US imports rather badly mostly in favour of low-cost (mostly British) reality shows.

One of the first shows which disappeared from Channel 4 after years of being faithfully shown on the weekends was *Stargate SG-1*. Back in 2006 as its last season approached, the show was poached by satellite TV giant Sky. Having missed out on the original, its spin-offs, *Stargate: Atlantis* and *Stargate: Universe* also went to other channels. This would be a taste of things to come as loyal viewers were left high and dry if they did not have Sky TV.

The next two programmes were *Alias*, staring Jennifer Garner as the super spy, and *Angel*, the *Buffy* spin-off. Channel 4 did not know when to schedule these two -tea time or primetime? They tried 4pm to 6pm slots, which didn't work and lo and behold, these two shows sunk, only for both to be picked up by [Channel] Five, which promptly shoved them into late night slots. After season two, *Alias* disappeared to a cable channel and Five never got to the last season of *Angel.* Were the ratings poor because Channel 4 placed them in dismal time slots or were they in those scheduling dead-spots because Channel 4 didn't know what to do with them? If Channel 4 cannot back shows then why procure them in the first place? It is a disingenuous policy to have shows, but not to advertise or back them adequately and then dump them.

The biggest loss to Channel 4 was *Lost*. The battle for *Lost* was won by Sky after two seasons on the terrestrial channel. Money had won out and fans were left fuming, again, having to switch their loyalties from one channel to another. Luckily, the DVD market has made such channel transitions easier to avoid. That was a big-time hit to Channel 4, but things are still wobbly on the import front.

The latest two shows to feel Channel 4's loss of love are *Ugly Betty* and *Desperate Housewives*. Both shows were high-flyers anchoring primetime schedules. But as soon as it was announced that *Ugly Betty* had been cancelled in the US, Channel 4 demoted *Ugly Betty* to Sunday lunchtime viewing (with repeats on Saturdays). And for no apparent reason *Desperate Housewives* was taken from its coveted 9pm mid-week slot to a Sunday 10pm time. Channel 4's lack of faith in such programmes has been utterly exposed as a string of cheesy UK-made shows take the place of quality shows. One can only fear for the likes of *True Blood*, *The Good Wife*, and *The Event*. Consider Five's almost religious-like commitment to the *CSI* and *NCIS* franchises and you get the picture.

Also in contrast, is Channel 4's attachment to endless repeats of US comedies. *Friends, Fraiser, Will & Grace, Everybody Loves Raymond,* and *According to Jim*, among others are ubiquitous early morning staples. Yet, even in their primetime heyday *Friends, Fraiser*, and *Will & Grace* retained their slots and endless runs. Of course, half-hour comedies are cheaper to produce and buy, but Channel 4 did not tinker with their schedules or drop the shows. Channel 4 just seems to be bereft of ideas in how to deal with their hour-long US imports.

This cannot be just about ratings and money. While Channel 4 is a commercial station there is still a duty to reciprocate viewers' allegiances. But Channel 4 shows no such loyalty to its viewers. Yes, the cost of producing shows has gone up, the recession has hit, and internet and satellite competition are fierce, but other channels have shown far more consistency in its programming. Channel 4 programmers just don't seem to care about the quality of their channel.

There may also be a cultural element involved. Some British viewers argue that it is good that US imports are given short-shrift, because they are more violent than UK shows, too jingoistic, and shallow, even though the general quality of US programmes have risen. But it is not the quality of US imports that is the matter; it is Channel 4's policy of changing the schedules of shows or discontinuing their runs against viewers' wishes or prior knowledge, thereby breaking viewer loyalty and destroying any trust in Channel 4.

One can only hope that Channel 4 starts to view its US programmes like prized gems. At the moment, they are treated like monopoly pieces and moved randomly from high-valued slots to down-market spots, not befitting their brand. It's time for Channel 4 to stop rolling the dice, for one day the gamble with viewers' TV experiences will leave Channel 4 itself out-scheduled and losers in the TV game.

21/Nov/2011

Entertainment - TV genres

The End of Doctor Who?

2020 vision
Well the truth was out recently in the episode 'The Timeless Children' with the 13th Doctor. Was I close?

Doctor Who? That was the question which was left to linger in the minds of viewers from the episode 'The Wedding of River Song', the last of the 2011 series. Of course the question has always been there, but the latest Doctor Who series, beginning with the revamped Christopher Eccleston era, has focussed more on the Doctor's background such as his life on Gallifrey, his relationship to his mortal frenemy The Master, and hints at having a family.

Matt Smith is the 11th incarnation of the Doctor, viewers knowing that the Doctor only has thirteen lives in total. When we first met the Doctor in 1963, he was an elderly grandfather (to Susan – another mysterious character) who now seems to be leading a Benjamin-Buttonesque life with every successive regeneration. We knew nothing of his past, except that he stole the Tardis to escape Gallifrey's inward-looking existence. Along with the Doctor, the Master, the Rani, and the Corsair, were also renegade Time Lords with stolen time-travelling property voyaging the universe for their own purposes.

For such a major character, to not know the Doctor's past never seems to have mattered to viewers. There had been hints about what he was running away from and suggestions of a family life with the aforementioned granddaughter Susan. But whether she was an actual blood relative wasn't made clear. The Doctor does have a daughter, named Jenny, 'manufactured' in 2008's episode 'The Doctor's Daughter' where she proved her Time Lord capabilities by regenerating. Recently, it was even thought that he was the sole remaining Time Lord –he still might be. But the Doctor has always been focussed on the future, everyone else's, rather than his own past. So we are no nearer to finding out who he is.

But is this about to change? There were hints at the end of last season that as the Doctor nears the end of his regenerations we would finally find out who he is. There is a myth that the Doctor's real name is a secret that must never be revealed or "Silence will fall when the question is asked." This foretells that knowing the Doctor's name would have drastic consequences. But what's in a name? What is the Silence –peace or the end of everything? And even if the question is asked, who says there has to be an answer? Do we really want or need to know? Surely such a story would be an anti-climax.

What could possibly be revealed? What tragedy (for it would have to be one to complete the Doctor's life circle) will the Doctor bring upon the universe if his true identity was discovered? Why is his name a secret? Surely other Time Lords must have known it. If they did not know then why not? Will we hear or see the Doctor's back story in TV flashback or in what has been recently announced a new Doctor Who big-screen adventure? This would be the only way to end Doctor Who's story or he would forever remain a mysterious stranger with only his future that counts.

Could the Doctor be Omega, the creator of the Time Lord technology, but in a different incarnation? Omega and Rassilon created the black hole (The Eye of Harmony) and Time Lord technology, respectively. The Doctor may know a secret or be a special outcome of this event. The Doctor could be Alpha. If Omega began the Time Lords, then surely Alpha would end them. The Doctor did trap Rassilon and the Time Lords during the Last Great Time War against the Daleks. And with the Master's help seemingly destroyed them. The Doctor has always seemed too prescient, even for a Time Lord. Maybe he had seen the future of the Time Lords and what they would do to the universe. This special ability may mark the Doctor as a new type of Time Lord; a bridge between old and new Time Lord regimes.

And what role does Earth play? Is there a master plan behind the Doctor's fascination with Earth? The Doctor has the whole of universe and time to roam yet spends most of his time on Earth or around humans. Is this really out of love for humanity or is there a deeper link to Gallifrey? This could be the crux of the story. The Doctor may practice non-violence himself, but as has been noted by many an adversary, the Doctor is not averse to recruiting his own army of humans who have sacrificed themselves for his ideals over the years.

The Doctor's end would have to involve Gallifrey and Earth. Gallifrey or Earth could be the progenitor of the other or Earth could succeed Gallifrey. The Doctor has been watching over Earth to make that happen. In an over-wrought cliché, the Doctor could be 'The One' of 'The Chosen One' to build a new Time Lord society on Earth.

There can be no doubt that the Doctor is an omniscient, omnipotent, omnipresent character. But he is not God. The Doctor is probably an aspect or relative of Omega or he is the opposite of Omega: Alpha the end of the Time Lords and the beginning of something new, perhaps with Earth poised to take over the mantle of time guardians of the universe. So, who is the Doctor? We simply don't know, but we hope that when the Silence falls the Doctor will be there to make it all better.

Poems

15/May/1998

I Faltered

I faltered with every breath of my soul
Resisting stars so wondrously bright, those wintry nights
Beckoned by air to cool inspired heights.
I reached the peak, no going back, and I faltered after all.

I faltered. Couldn't save myself from the fall
Too many steps to climb, so far to go
My strength failed me. I never felt so low
I reached the peak, no going back, and I faltered after all

I'm falling down the world, no time to stop
Falling in Oblivion, hell's no bother, it's a further drop
I'm falling down the world, straight from the top

I faltered, but I'm coming back from the edge
Battered and bruised, I had fallen astray
But I'm fighting back, I'm finding my way
I reached the peak, no going back, and I faltered
But that's life, after all.

17/May/1998

My Lady

Fierce eyes
They scared me, they burned me,
they scorched me, they raked me
naked – they saw right through me
Bone to my soul, down in my hole
Fierce eyes

Cold smile
Froze me under ice-like winter's glare
Moody lips of blue without a care
Snow down, snow frown
Emotion flaking under skin
Hidden deep in frost within

Hard heart
Never knew a beat that did not hate
Once of diamond, but no jewel of late
Love could find no purchase in that mine
Stripped of all its precious veins through wine

I never knew you could smile
Together forever, loveless, faithless
I never thought I'd see you smile
Now I'm dying, pain and crying
And you're smiling, smiling, smiling
Now you're smiling
Smiling, smiling
My lady

29/Jan/2008

Stars

Do stars cry in the middle of the star-lit night
about life, death and the loneliness of light?

Are they sentient and sensitive to the screams of the void within which they swim upon gravity buoyed?

Are they proud of their magnitude, their velocity and hue as they peer down at vacuum from which particles spew?

Can they see the dimensions invisible to those
who don't have the energy to see beyond their nose?

Are they scared of the holes as black as death
which actually exhale the faintest of breath?

Do they play upon the dust of the newborns
and sing along to the chorus of the new dawn?

Oh, why stars can't you share your memories,
your thoughts, and your views with us mere mortals who would love to hear your news?

So, don't you stars cry to the universe for feeling so alone spare a thought for us humans, it's all we've ever known!

17/Dec/2008

Christmas poem – Money and Energy

Christmas 2008

***

Money and energy:
It's the focus of the year;
swirling all around us, draining away.
Has hit us all in various ways and so come Christmas day,
the yearly goodwill I've saved
will be spent on virtual yuletide trade.

***

Of course, you are worth much more than mere money;
You supply the vital energy of priceless
and endless friendship to me,
You empower me through the crunchy recession we now see.

***

So a very merry and prosperous Christmas to you.
And thank you for enriching my life
beyond any bailout could afford in true.
Here's to '09, happier climes, and a time to start anew.

***

Blessings and Wishes, always, my friends!

17/Apr/2009

Happy Birthday, Sis!

*

You're a Butterfly
flying high on destiny's wings
blossoming into a woman of all things.

The magic 40 had been achieved
and, oh, what a wonderful life you have weaved.

Daughter, sister, wife, and mother,
I wouldn't wish for anyone other

*

Love, big brother xx

04/Jun/2009

Poetry of wine

Happy birthday to a fine-aged wine lover
of red, white, mulled, or other.
You're a connoisseur true of the grape-wine fodder,
a long way from the milk of your mother.

*

Chocolates, diamonds, roses, and cheeses
pale in comparison to a wine that pleases.
So at your party of tricks and teases,
choose a wine that's the bees'es knees'es

*

So sip, don't swill, and drink responsibly,
'tis a lady's chance to end the night nobly.
A vintage year will come to be,
for a fine-aged lover of wine and me.

12/Dec/2009

Real One

She can rip your heart out with her eyes
So brown, so deep, so lingeringly sweet

She can rend your soul apart with her smile
So warm, so lovely, and rosy-red cheeked

She makes me mind-numbingly weak
Shivering from awe in her wake

She is beauty, she is care
She trills with a grace of heart-swelling degree

I daren't say her name for fear of breaking the spell
breathtakingly cast on me when I first glimpsed her to be.

Shall I whisper her name? Nay!
To the universe I will proclaim
That she is everything I seek
Perfect, sensual, magnifique

Yet, I have named her:
Real One
A twist in the words
She knows I dream of her and wait
For I am wrecked upon her wow-inspiring ship of state

Nevertheless, I shall remain silent in tone
For to her, I am neither real nor the one

24/Dec/2009

*

A Christmas Dream

It's that time of year
to reflect upon what has come to pass.
But let us also look toward
the golden future's looking glass.

This year, I stood perilously upon the cusp
of realising my dream,
but even if fate has only allowed me to peer
though the magic door without entering in esteem
at least I have seen the potential within me
and the best I can still achieve.

And so unto you, my friends, if you still have a dream,
If you still stand unbowed and steadfast in determination
to attain your heart's desire
then let 2010 become your year of fulfilment and ever higher.

My Christmas Wish this year
is for each and every one of us to grasp our dreams
To be more than we are; to be what we want to be,
no matter the route or how long it takes.
A dream is forever, not just for Christmas
Don't throw it away. Never forget it!
Strive for it, take it, live it.
Be the dream….

15/Feb/2010

Ode to M: She no play bongo

*

Out one night and he played to the beat
for the girl he liked
he thought it was sweet.
But his bongo didn't go down a treat.

In a tale regaled, she wanted him to know
how a man had tried to teach her to bongo.
But short on time her answer was "no",
"What's in it for me? What's in it for you?"
"Nowt" said he – and disinterested was she,
so sad for the maestro that she no play bongo.

Crestfallen your teller of this tale he was
for deep affection for the no-wanna-bongo lass he professed.
Bongo is a way of life,
no matter the beat and how long it lasts.
Better to play bongo and lost
than never to play bongo at all, he jest.

There would have been the memories
and foundation for future revelries.
But now they'll never know –for she is soon gone.
And for your poor maestro she no play bongo.

18/Apr/2010

Let Me Be

Your smile once enlightened me
Your eyes brought me clarity
Your voice commanded me
Your laughter refreshed me

~

But now wash me away with your tears
I won't miss you.
Smother me with your cries of despair
I won't hear you.
I won't break
I am a mountain of hardened stone
A soul made of stuff to be alone.

~

Your touch will burn me
Your breath will deaden me
I am buried under your presence
Leave me
Forswear me
Forget me.

~

Let me be

13/Jan/2010

Climatic Dramatics

Eyes are the windows into the soul,
but windows are the eyes into solar power.
All along the watchtowers
of skyscrapers, houses, and all through the hours,
trade windows for sun panels to meet our energy goal.

Beauty is in the eye of the beholder,
but we are beholden to ugly fossil fuels
for all our glamorous needs.
Our beautiful Gaia stripped of valuable jewels
all for our vainglorious greed.

But waste not, want not;
cradle to cradle resources are getting hot.
The future will run on spoils,
gobbled from our copious heaps,
and harvested from what we sow, we reap.

Every cloud has a silver lining,
especially when fed from a hydrogen cell
to deflect Global Warming's barrage.
Cleaner fuel and cooler air will tell
enough to reject the sceptic's mirage.

Does a tree make a sound when it falls in the forest,
even if it is artificial?
Whether scrubbing carbon or pumping underground
more trees please before we drown
in the rising tides of our man-made interglacial.

Old MacDonald had a farm
of turbines and fish on the side.
With batteries of fish for chips and pie
and selling the excess back to the grid,
the only time water and electricity mix.

To be or not to be?
That's Humanity's ultimate question
of survival or extinction.
With so much around us in nature and technology
surely we'll succeed and live life Carbon neutrally.

04/Dec/2011

Heart Void

I tried to put my heart into play again.
Love loosened and on the line.
Thought I had found The One for all time
after so long on the wane.

Yet there was no connection.
I am shut down like a machine,
flirtations with emotions rarely seen.
No sense of empathy. No powers of attraction.

Now she's a relic from my past.

For I am a void
Destined to be alone
I like to be alone
Crave to be alone
Leave me alone

I will switch off hope's radar for a while.
Drift through the entangled social firmament,
like a ship on the high seas of abandonment
in a dark and cold and hopeless wild.

I will seek no port, shun all harbours, steer no course,
an embraceless life away from others.
Why wreck myself against another?
Weigh anchor and cross the feeling horizon,
for I shall not cross love's latitude again.

Lash me to the unkindest mast
if the siren's call should lure me to shore.
To have loved and lost, I want no more
For this man's heart is a void to the last.

18/Nov/2013

The Isolation Gene

The isolation gene.
It exists.
It twists
in the gut and the brain
Forbidding the curse of companionship again.

The isolation gene
It's instinct.
It's linked
When the heart breaks
And the soul aches.

It kicks into gear
To protect one from love
When it hurts with another
who does not love you back.

The isolation gene
Keeps you safe from harm
A self-protection charm
Against stepping into pain.

So don't ignore it
Don't fight it or forget this
It evolves and loves you in a way unseen
The isolation gene.

Projects

28.10.02

PROJECT 2

2020 Vision

While some of my articles, songs, and poems pre-dated my Helium days, I also had other literary projects on the go. I was reminded of one such grand project when I recently saw a book called *The Poems of a Modern-day Architect* by Aline Chahine. I was like 'Hey, I had a similar idea' incorporated into a larger work. I hunted it down in my files. And here it is below. Maybe one day I may finish the project completing poems for the other buildings and adding in such new luminary buildings such as the Shard, Fenchurch Street's Walkie Talkie building, the Arcelor Mittal Tower, the Heron Tower, the Razor at Elephant & Castle, etc. So many buildings to eulogise and write poems about.

Not sure what Project 1 was, but this must have been the follow up. Probably to do with photography, as I was and still am interested in architecture and photographing buildings.

My Project 2 book has the subtitle 'Modern Monumental Architecture of London' and also a plan to introduce the subject of 'Geological Architecture': Getting to know what the buildings are made of, making a 'stratigraphical layout of the building' or a geological recipe. In short I wanted to know all about the buildings, their names, dimensions, location (plotted on London map), a short history with urban archaeologists musings, what were their construction materials and sourcing, and what their purpose was.

I wanted to know if buildings were aligned to the cardinal points. I used archaeological factors to look at modern buildings. Of course they weren't used as tombs, but they still were based on hierarchial factors with the bosses at top, traditionally closer to the gods and away from the rabble.

It would also be interesting to know about the architects' thoughts, if certain parameters were conscious or unconscious decisions about certain building traditions. Why are some buildings pilgrimage sites or ceremonial centres rather than others built for that purpose. It's like physics where elegant mathematics, equations and solutions are seen as more truthful than 'ugly', ungainly ones. Humans like beauty in whatever they see or build and monumental buildings, especially the beautifully crafted ones are still as fascinating to us now as they were when they first touched the sky millennia ago.

I had divided this work into 4 sections:

Monolithica
Glass Menageries
Towers and Circles
Edifaces and Complexes

There were probably going to be more, but the project ended most probably due to work, start of another project or loss of interest.

Monolithica

Some people don't like Skyscrapers
The pyramids of the 20th Century and beyond
Edifaces of commerce, workers buried beneath mounds of paper
The hands of time ticking away like the desert sands.
How long will their walls last?

Index:
Tower 42
International Press Centre
Centre Point
Canary Wharf
City Point

Tower 42

Is Big necessarily beautiful?
Tower 42 is there, erect and proud
A functional thoughtful, serenely benign observer.
If it were alive it'd be a leaf-eating giant
grazing on the fruits of the city

Centre Point

A marker in the rivers of commerce
beacon for the lost travellers of life

City Point

A glass mast in a sea of buildings
with a crow's nest watching the financial horizon
A helmsmen's centre in a ship of commerce
Steady as she goes.

*

Glass Menageries

Index:
Swiss Re (30 St. Mary's Axe)/The Gherkin
Great Court, British Museum
Sainsburys HQ (33 High Holborn)
Moorhouse (Moorgate)
GLA (Greater London Authority) Building

The Gherkin

Pillar of Insurance
Neither Ionian, Doric, or Corinthian
Sexy bit of fast food nobody wants

Moorhouse

An unacclaimed Foster Building
A glassy gate along the City Wall
in the shadow of taller points
But a classy substrate curves and all.

*

Towers and Circles

Remnants of lost Battlements and Observatories

Index:
BT Tower
London Eye
St. Brides Chapel ('The Fleet Street Wedding Cake')

The London Eye

Stonehenge on edge
in the mould of yore
spoked-lintel revolutions
entertaining evolution
No starry collusion
on the Millennium Wheel
just a celestial phenomenon
a new age monument

*

Edifaces and Complexes

City Cliffs and Cities in Miniature

Index:

MI6 Building

Fortress with a bond to the past
A battlement of secrets

Goldman Sachs -Peterborough Court & Rivercourt

From vintage Art Deco to a visionary echo
like a Borg cube linked to its finer brother
by celestial bridges of finance
where men of gold earn their sachs of money
investing all on a street fleet with power.

*

THE NON-CONFORMIST

THE NON-CONFORMIST

H

E

N

O

N

-

C

O

N

F

O

R

M

I

S

T

THE NON-CONFORMIST

THE

NON-CONFORMIST

THE NON-CONFORMIST

THE NON-CONFORMIST

THE NON-CONFORMIST

T

H

E

N

O

N

-

C

O

N

F

O

R

M

I

S

T

Conceived 09.08.08

2020 vision

Opposite is the cover page for a project I conceived in 2008. There is concerted pressure by 'society' to make their fellow citizens conform with the idea of having to get married, start a family, have the car, house, high tech gadgets (including a fridge), job for life, etc. But that is not for everyone. So, I decided to celebrate non-conformist people with a print and/or online magazine. At first, the magazine was about non-conformist (whatever that means nowadays as normal is a relative term and everyone is a non-conformist in their own right). Then I sought to focus it on singledom, but the scattershot approach combining both didn't quite work out the way I wanted. However, the magazine would have been a great way for non-conformists and singletons to navigate the world with a zine specifically for them.

Non*Conformist Magazine

Definition:

http://query.nytimes.com/search/query?srchst=ref&query=The Nonconformist &fw=1 (link no longer active)

Why is there a stigma attached to being single well into later life? Some people think that it is almost socially unacceptable to be alone, or wanting to be childless. They feel such people cannot be happy and try to talk them around and fix them up with partners.

Non*conformist Magazine is a collective shout from the so-called loners and free-thinkers of society: 'Leave us alone!' We really are happy as we are; single, independent, and living our own lives.

Non*conformist will strive to make sense of the emerging trends in nonconformist living, seeing what's best for you, being happy and assessing the reality of the nonconformist community.

Vive the Nonconformist!

Editorial:

21st Century Caveman:

What is there for a man to do in the New Age of New Men, Metrosexuals, Mannies and the political correct. This is not about sexist or misogynist attitudes, but about men coming together to voice their views about their world; the non-conformist, independent, single men who want to hold onto the caveman within themselves.

The caveman is a man of a certain age who should be married with kids, mortgaged to the hilt, juggling a business career and having nights out with the lads (when permitted by the missus), but that was not their path.

The caveman is the eternal bachelor, a solitary dreamer, a hunter for new ideas, a fighter for his way of life, who is happy or feels happiness through individual pursuits. This magazine encompasses those ideals for those who would rather eschew what 'organised civilisation' has to offer and to think for themselves.

This is for the non-committed, wanting no responsibility, for the single, active man seeking challenges in life; the asexual, the Spurmos (Straight, Proud, Unmarried men over 30), the jack of all trades, drifters, self-entrepreneurs, free-thinkers, 'Regretful Loners' and those of the Menaissance, whether in life, business or entertainment.

The Singles Advocate:
News for the Nonconformists:
What issues do singles and other nonconformists think about? Well the same thing as everyone else, but the Singles Advocate will filter out news from TV and print media and relate them to you. If there are initiatives that affect a singleton's world, like taxes, health or free time, then you will have the news and analyses of how it will affect you, and what you can do. The Singles Advocate also lets the readers tell their own stories and set the agenda for discussions and debates.

Examples of feature articles:
Men:
SPURMOs:
http://www.timesonline.co.uk/tol/life_and_style/men/article4008461.ece (link no longer active)
www.spurmo.com (Link no longer active)

Regretful Loners:
http://www.guardian.co.uk/commentisfree/story/0,,1837771,00.html
(Link active as of October 2020)

Menassaince – the rebirth of Men:
http://www.gfwadvertiser.ca/index.cfm?sid=62181&sc=294 (link no longer active)

http://www.socyberty.com/Men/Menaissance-The-Rebirth-of-Man.62884 (link no longer active)

Youth:

The Quarter-life crisis:
http://www.boston.com/news/globe/living/articles/2004/09/08/the_quarter_life_crisis/ (link active as of October 2020)
There are the 20-somethings on the brink of conformity after university, choosing either the security of a job with attendant marriage, mortgage, or a life less ordinary full of debt. But some of them choose to be non-conformist setting up their own businesses or following their own way of life. The Quarter-life Crisis could be the catalyst for change and success rather than a depressing period of life.

Yeppies:
Related to the Quarter-life crisis are the Yeppies (Young Experimenting Perfection Seekers), the 16-24 year olds who are not yet materialistic, but shop around for experience, dipping in and out of the job market, testing and tasting bits of what life has to offer before settling down. Is this a symptom, a sign, of the Quarter-life Crisis starting or breaking? Is there too much choice on offer, which confuses or turns off those to working? Does the rise of 'prolonged adolescence' lead to underachievers? Or are Yeppies creating and experiencing their own tailor-made gap years to get the best out of life? This next generation will be setting our future agendas. Let's hope they make the right choices.

Issues to discuss:

Short articles on nonconformist attitudes to life, teaching, exercising, eating, socialising, religion, sex, politics, etc.

Uncommon People: The Nonconformist Community is made up of a myriad of people. Some want to be different, but others are unconventional through no choice of their own. Society can spoil people, make them less trusting, prone to violence and open to indoctrination into the 'orthodox' culture. Nonconformists seek to avoid or mitigate the negatives of society by being different. Uncommon People takes a look at those who lives are different because of our adverse society.

Pros and Cons of being a nonconformist? Is there a true nonconformist lifestyle?

Where are the polymaths, the iconoclasts and the visionaries? Where are the genius of multiple disciplines; the (mad) scientists and boffins who dabble in everything and contribute a wealth of information across societal bonds?

How to teach children how to think, to be creative and independent? Home-schooling and other methods of teaching non-curriculum, but important social skills.

Married Nonconformists: Can't live with them; can't live without them - The phenomenon of living in separate houses, having separate lives; but in an exclusive relationship or marriage. Does absence make the heart grow fonder?

Is one's own privacy really a ticket to personal freedom?

Are some people 'primed' into a default state of living alone?

Is marriage just now one of many 'disposable experiences'?

Downshifting: Why sacrifice career commitments for a better quality of life? What makes someone leave a top city job for the country or from being a Trader to a tradesman? Is this a nonconformists shift or a hidden trend dredge up by the media? Is there such a thing as the Good Life? Have intrinsic values started to seep into society? Can anyone downshift and what options are there when downshifting? This is Downshifting made simple. http://en.wikipedia.org/wiki/Simple_living. (link active as of October 2020)

Protirement: the ultimate downshifting for the already well-off. They are the working hobbyists who have retreated from salaried work at an early age, sold off everything and moved on to a simpler life pursuing personal pleasures sustained by the resultant proceeds or from an inheritance. It's a high risk proactive lifestyle for the youthful post-work brigade.
http://www.workingsenior.com/cm/Newletter/ReferencedFiles/June%2007/Think%20Protirement%20Not%20Retirement.html
(link no longer active).

Maturialism: From the baby boomer generation of non-conformists come the big spenders of a certain age not yet ready to retire gently into the night. They want to experience life in good health and wealth, eschewing leaving an inheritance or having already left a pre-inheritance to the

children. Is it a case of a second childhood or signs of a late mid-life crisis? If you can't take it with you, then why not spend it on happiness and 'affluenze' your friends as well. Is there a darker side to this with advertising and marketing agencies driving this product frenzy and seizing you in your twilight years and cashing in?
http://www.timesonline.co.uk/tol/comment/columnists/guest_contributors/article534567.ece (Link no longer active).

Are SKIers (parents who Spend the Kids' Inheritance) right in their choice? Is there any imperative to leave anything for your children in this day and age?

Deconstructing the Nonconformist: 'Once people are encouraged to redefine themselves, they need goods and services to help them construct their new identities' (Thompson 2008: 124). Therefore, nonconformists are still tied into the consumerist machine and nonconformity may just be another subset of consumer labelled for new products and marketing industries. Discuss!

Features and Columns:
Meal for One: We'll turn this normally pejorative phrase into a celebration of eating healthily and thrift-fully. Quick meals, what's best on the market, bargains, tips for cooking, tips for the tricky single eater, and even a guide to the best types of take-aways. Basically, the beginners guide to having a great singles life in the kitchen. Men need never be afraid of the kitchen again!

Solo Pound: The best value for money deals for holidays, travel, restaurants and other singles packages. What are the effects of singles on the housing markets, the auto industry and other trades? Does the single spender still make a difference in the economy?

The Insider: Outside life isn't that good for some, so what do these sun-shy, curtain- twitching, couch potatoes do all day or night besides surf, eat, and watch TV? We reveal the life of the Urban Hermit and their reasons for staying indoors. We also chart the rise and popularity of the cyber nonconformists or the non-econoformists, those economically tied to work-from-home schemes either with their company, as independent contractors/freelancers, or as hobbyists for extra money. Basically, at home with the nonconformists.

Individual Health: Singles, especially men between 25 and 44, are accused of not visiting the doctor often enough, leading to more cases of depression, heart disease and emotional problems. Here, ways to work out at home, work or a gym are laid out with guides to nutritional ways to supplement physical workouts. There will also be guides to common ailments and advice on how to deal with symptoms, including dreaded visits to the doctor.

Single Minded: Related to Individual Health, what is the psychology behind being single? How to avoid being stuck in an overtly 'me, me, me' mode, or becoming anti-social or feeling overwhelmingly alone. Great ways to make yourself feel happy, worthwhile and getting over tough times. How to be successful at singledom and survive the machinations of match-maker friends. The Art of Being Single and Happy.

Greens Only: The single's life of being green. Are singles more energy-efficient or wasteful than their coupled companions? How can singles save energy and money and become more resourceful and resilient as the credit crunch hits? Tips from readers on how to be more green. Nonconformist ways of becoming and staying green and energy resourceful.

The Non-Conformissus: For the discerning single woman and the non-Bridget Jones types who is a conformist-in-waiting. We're looking for the 'free spirits', the Biological Clockless, the un-broody, the Wiccas and the Gay Divorcees. Many Women are happy alone and feel no guilt in having no children, or raising kids with no steady man in their lives, and the freedom to run their lives and business their own way. They are the self-taught, savvy women who escaped from the world of the ladettes and the Boardroom. Celebrate your lives here!

New York Times article from a mother to a daughter:

http://www.nytimes.com/2007/07/01/magazine/01wwln-lede-t.html?fta=y (link active as of October 2020)

Single Scene: Sex life of the nonconformist. How to meet people, have fun, and stay unattached. Sex tips and toys, the dating scene, and night life. Maintaining a carefree single's lifestyle. Uncovering the asexual and living without the need or urge for sex.

One On One: The Interview. A chosen single or nonconformist will be interviewed (hopefully a celebrity or successful person) and what they think of their non-conformist life and the world around them. Inspiring thoughts and views!

Projects:

Mapping:
With all the data from ONS, would it be possible to map and plot the distribution of the nonconformists in Britain and predict future trends? Would be great for GIS!!

Trend setter:
Analysing the words used to describe groups of nonconformists; coming up with new words, and scanning the future for upcoming nonconformist trends.
http://trendwatching.com/ (link active as of October 2020)

Future Projects?
Synthetics –the otherworld nonconformists. Would be good to have an Avatar from online world such as World of Warcraft, The Sims, or Second Life comment upon why their world is better than ours, the nonconformist movements within them and if/how they affect our real world.

Futurologists: By definition are probably nonconformists dreaming of the world to come and making it happen. How much will Transhumanism and the Singularity affect our world and the way we see ourselves when technology becomes a part of human than biology? Will non-conformity transcend the human phase?

Books and Reviews:

Books on *Nonconformists*: (links active as of October 2020)

Anthony Storr: *Solitude*: http://www.amazon.com/Solitude-Return-Self-Anthony-Storr/dp/0345358473

Books on the Quarter-life Crisis:
http://www.amazon.co.uk/s/ref=nb_ss_w_h_/203-5685010-6699140?url=search-alias%3Dstripbooks&field-keywords=quarter+life+crisis

Books on Downshifting:
http://www.amazon.co.uk/s/ref=nb_ss_w_h_/203-5052307-0014346?url=search-alias%3Daps&field-keywords=downshifting

Questions and Answers:
Nonconformist 'experts' answer questions from readers about life.

Odd jobs and ads:
Jobs for the nonconformist, whether unsociable hours jobs, contract work, creative enterprises, events and meetings. Advertisements from other nonconformist companies, individuals and sponsors.

NON*CONFORMIST STRUCTURE

Writers and contributors:
Be nice to have mostly non-experts leading the way, people who live these lives and can write about it, which will lend authenticity to the title. Many articles may be from readers giving a greater voice to the Nonconformists and singles of Britain.

Articles:
Monthly hardcopy magazine with online 'shadow'.
Feature articles (3-4 pages)
Short articles and stories (1 page or less)
Rotating features depending on availability of writers and interest.

NON*CONFORMIST ONLINE

(Website only option)

Nonconformist Online (NonConOn) would be a web-only based site bringing together all aspects of the nonconformist lifestyle. Based on a loose Helium.com model readers and writers would be able to register for free their own personal page, to write articles on any subject to do with being nonconformist, and get paid for it.

Alternatively, NonConOn could be a free knowledge sharing site, though I am a fan of the idea that intellectual property should be paid for. After all, ideas will be the next big thing!!

Articles would have a minimum word limit of at least 300 words as comments and blogs could be posted on separate forum pages. Officially there would be no upper limit, though over long articles would be sorted through a rating system, which would be a blind system, so no names are shown and higher rated articles get paid more.

Helium also has a Steward system where people –like myself- are selected to 'police' our respective title channels and sub channels making sure that writing standards are up to scratch and people are not abusing the system, in other words –making sure they conform! [ironic]. NonConOn would have a similar system though due to our more nonconformist natures would have a more tolerant approach towards subjects and title content. More severe abuses could be dealt with according to provisions in Terms and Conditions and other writing standard agreements.

Again, due to our nonconformist nature, articles may or may not be grouped together under over-arching titles, though a search facility will be included. Titles can be added by the 'powers-that-be' or by writers. All the subjects discussed above for the proposed magazine would be online article titles with sub titles spinning off them. The titles will not be gender specific in that each one can write about the other, gaining insights into what each gender thinks about the other's nonconformist issues.

To complete the site, the 'Singles Advocate' would be the front page 'news channel' keeping people up to date with all their noncon news and views. Portals would also lead to other linked sites, especially for advertisers and job opportunities.

Like Helium, NonConOn would be a knowledge-sharing network, the ultimate one-stop shop for all your nonconformist needs. No need to check separate websites, books, magazines and newspapers, or other sources, NonConOn would have all of this and more.

Possible article titles:

Defining your Nonconformity:
Each nonconformist can write about their own issues through several titles.
What are the pros and cons of being a single man or woman?
What are the pros and cons of being nonconformists?

The 21st Century Caveman: Old Age man is back. But can he survive in the modern world?
Are SPURMOs an endangered species?
Are you a Regretful Loner?
Do you feel guilty over your decisions as a singleton?
Celebrating the Menaissance: Will the Return of The Man change our society?
Are you suffering a Quarter-life crisis? And ways to conquer it.
Are the Yeppies the way forward for the next generation?
Ways to avoid total indoctrination into a conformist society
Why do we have no more celebrated polymaths?
Who are the Visionaries for the 21st Century?
How to teach children to think for themselves and why this is important.
Can't live with them; can't live without them: Married singletons.
Are some people primed into a default state of living alone?
Is marriage now just one of many 'disposable experiences'?
Downshifting: Why sacrifice your career for a better quality of life?
Is there such a thing as an easy Protirement?
Are the Maturialists selfish people?
Are SKIers depriving their children of a better future?
Deconstructing the nonconformist: Are we just another brand?
Meal for One: The ins and outs of eating alone.
Solo Pound / Dollar: Are singletons good value for money?
How to be a productive Urban Hermit
How to make money as an econoformist?
How to stay physically healthy as a singleton
Me, myself and I: Staying mentally fit as a singleton
How to be single and happy
Can you be single and green?
The nonconformissus: How not to be a Bridget Jones
Is the biological clock a useless mechanism?
Why the urge to brood isn't all it's cracked up to be.
Guide to free spirits: How to be independent and unrepentant.
Sex and the single scene: Tell us all about it.
Being asexual in the modern age
What will the future of nonconformity be?
Who is more nonconformist –you or your virtual Avatar?
Who is you favourite nonconformist person?
Reviews of nonconformist products
Reviews of nonconformist books

And so much more, with variations and interpretations on titles and thousands of writers doing their own thing. Nonconformist Online, your ultimate source.

Whether a printed magazine or an online network, Non*Conformist will be a unique brand with a large and diverse customer base. As more people seek unconventional experiences and lifestyles they will want and need guidance, advice and an outlet for those experiences.

Non*Conformist can also pick up and analyse long-term trends or reveal the latest fads and marketing campaigns aimed at real or imagined nonconformist groups. We will assess whether the nonconformist brand is running its own course or is steered by the clever admen.

Non*Conformist: coming soon.

Songs

2020 Visions

I have no idea where the impulse to write songs came from. I love music and can hold a tune, so my own ears tell me, but I can't play any instruments (despite piano lessons at High School and from my dad, a piano tuner and church organ builder - and I once had a ubiquitous 'Learn to Play the Guitar' dvd on the shelf for a while). But putting together a song, combining the words and music in your head, and committing to paper and voice can be hard. Maybe it was boredom while working nightshifts in security, but I just had a flood of ideas and the music and words just flowed out. I suppose I have an album's worth here, but whether it sees the light of day is another thing. Any music producers among my readers give me a shout. Below are some brief notes from around half the songs.

**

Perpetual Sunlight:
I was sitting on the upper deck of a bus on my way to work through Stratford, London, and looking out the window. The sun was shining through and the words 'perpetual sunshine' just hit me. I wrote this song around it, changing 'sunshine' to 'sunlight'.

Imagine Mike Flowers (remember him?) and his big band pop sound? Well the music has that vibe. I actually sang the song for a couple of fellow security guards in the office and one of them said I sounded like the guy from The Lighthouse Family (Tunde Baiyewu). So put those two elements together and you have Perpetual Sunlight.

*

What is it About the Stars:
I call this song my 'Spice Girls' song as I could imagine them singing this, in their maturer guises, a choral eulogy. I ended up using this in one of my sci-fi novels.

*

The Sky Warrior Hymn:
This was written purely for my Starguards sci-fi novel as the Hymn of the Sky Warriors, defenders of Magna Aura. It's sung just before the enemy advances, like the company of soldiers before facing the Zulus. Think Welsh men's choir sound or Russian military anthem and you get the picture.

*

Baby Love:
My 'Robbie Wlliams' song. Belt this one out in despairing love!

*

Down, Vicki, Down:
I was out with some friends, one of them called Vicky. We were all having a laugh outside a pub and she suddenly grabbed my shoulder in excitement. I thought to myself 'wow, down girl!' and the song was born from there, though the song is smuttier than the actual friendly instinctual action!

*

Home is My Lifeline
Using my 'Lighthouse Family' voice and piano accompaniment, this is probably my favourite song. Part of it is used by a character in my Starguards novel as a reminder of her past.

*

Man With a Gun
This kind of reflects gun crime through the ages with the beginning and end of the song reflecting an Old West theme with a cowboy's harmonica leading into a modern lament with lashings of guitars and drums, and plea at the end.

17/May/1998

Songs: Destiny

Can't You See Me?

A storm of stars shall start the world
And bring about love's dreams.
Living for the days beyond,
a further future's seen.

Darker days have come before
to countries lost and been,
spreading sins and crosses
on an empty magazine.

[Chorus]
Can't you see me? Can't you see me?
searching through the skies.
I'm sailing 'round the universe
to be right by your side.
Destiny can't keep me from
the loving of your eyes,
or else I'll swear I'll ride this spaceship
'til the day I die.

Bring me something, water
to put out the silky sheen
of fire from the skies above,
love lessons in between

Journey with me to the centre
of my heaven, queen.
Drinking from the fountain
youth springs for eternity

[Chorus]

A storm of stars will end the world
And bring about death's dreams
Looking at the days long gone
A dusty past is seen

[Chorus]
Can't you see me? Can't you see me?
searching through the skies.
I'm sailing 'round the universe
to be right by your side.
Destiny can't keep me from
the loving of your eyes,
or else I'll swear I'll ride this spaceship
'til the day I die.

*

22/May/1998

Songs: Sunshine

Perpetual Sunlight

Perpetual sunlight / fills my vision
Perpetual sunlight / makes my head swim
Perpetual sunlight / leaves me wondrin'
Perpetual sunlight / what a world we live in

[chorus]
You don't know what you've got
'til the sun is full eclipsed by the moon
And the stars come out to groove

Perpetual sunlight / beams of pleasure
Perpetual sunlight / starry weather
Perpetual sunlight / leaves me feelin'
Perpetual sunlight / like I'm dreamin'

[chorus]
Then the sky turns back pretty blue

Winter never comes and the rains will hardly ever be due
No nightingales will sing for the night-time is replaced by shining

Perpetual sunlight / slumber away
Perpetual sunlight / my sleepy-eyed babe
Perpetual sunlight / on a bed of rainbows
Perpetual sunlight / dream forever

[chorus]
And the stars come out to groove

Winter never comes and the rains will hardly ever be due.
No nightingales will sing for the night-time is replaced by shining.

The darkness never stays for the sun will always come shining through....

Perpetual sunlight [whisper]...

***

23/Aug/1998

Songs: Stars

What is it about the stars?

What is it about the stars,
that shine so brightly upon your face?
Protect you from the veil of darkness.
What is it about the stars?

The stars, that burn so bright,
like a halo dancing 'round your head,
shining forth the way to paradise
What is it about the stars?
What is it about the stars?

The stars, embrace your soul,
spreading wondrous love, the sunlight radiant
from above, for all your days

[chorus]
What is it about the stars, the stars,
What is it about the stars, they love you so
What is it about the stars, the stars
What is it about the stars?

The stars, that grant you heaven's will.
No host of angels can compare
in all the starry fields.

What is it about the stars, the stars,
What is it about the stars, they bless you so
What is it about the stars, the stars
What is it about the stars?

The stars, they sing your praises
to all of those in highest places.
A cosmic chorus in unison

What is it about the stars, the stars,
What is it about the stars, they shine for you

What is it about the stars, they burn for you
What is it about the stars?
The stars, the stars, the stars, the stars….[fade]

***

27/Feb/2000

Songs: Military anthems

The Sky Warrior Hymn

An Air Force Anthem:
[A hearty male choir with organ accompaniment]

See horizons on the opening sky.
See the dawn sun rising in your eyes.
Air superior, we will not falter.
See horizons in the sky.

[Chorus]
To see Sky Warriors upon high.
To be Sky Warriors 'til we die.
For thee, forever we will fly.
To be Sky Warriors upon high.

See defenders of the darkening sky.
Blue on blue triumphant colours fly.
Storms will never blow in ill against us.
See defenders of the sky.

[Chorus]

[Organ solo]

See Sky Warriors in the sky maternal.
For Glory, Air, and hard-fought Victory.
We the children of the air eternal.
See Sky Warriors in the sky.

[Chorus]

***

17/Jan/2001

Songs: Don't go away

Baby Love

[Chorus]
Baby Love, oh sweet Baby Love
You wanna leave me all alone,
you're gonna leave me, oh sweet Baby Love,
Oh sweet Baby Love,
you're gonna leave me all alone
for the rest of our lives.

**

I can't let you go tomorrow
not even for a day.
My heart cannot live without you
oh Baby Love please stay.
My soul's always yearning for you,
don't you go away.
All I do is for you baby
Oh Baby Love please stay, oh Baby Love please stay....
Oh whoa oh whoa, oh sweet Baby Love....

*

[chorus]

**

No one can foresee the paths
our tangled futures bring.
We will always be together,
through summer's sun 'til spring.
No two hearts were meant to be
apart indefinitely.
Only they can beat as one
for all eternity, for all eternity....
Oh whoa oh whoa, oh sweet Baby Love....

*

[chorus]

**

Forget all our stormy quarrels.
Remember all our dreams.
No more broken promises
or teary-eyed sad scenes
I can give you everything
your heart has been desirin'
Just whisper those sweet words to me
Tell me you won't go
Oh Baby Love please stay,
Oh whoa oh whoa, oh sweet Baby Love

*

[final chorus]
Baby Love, oh sweet Baby Love
You wanna leave me all alone
You're gonna leave me, oh sweet Baby Love
Singing Baby Love,
I'll always love you, Baby Love
for the rest of our lives,
You're gonna leave me all alone.
You're gonna leave me all alone.
For the rest of our lives,
you're gonna leave me all alone…..

*

Oh, baby, please don't go.

***

17/Jun/2005

Songs: Crazy love

Down, Vicki, Down

[guitar intro]

*

Met her on a winter's day.
Knew it straight away, I was captivated.
She bathed me in her radiant charm.
Only one problem, was a ring on her finger.

**

Tried to think away the pain,
of having my beloved belonging to another.
But she never went away,
she wanted me to come and play.
And I said:

[Chorus]
Down, Vicki, down,
Down, down, Vicki, down, down, down, down,
Down, down, Vicki, down
Down, down, Vicki, down

*****

Saw me in a corner café
She talked away for hours, had fun, fun, fun, fun.
She wanted to extend the meal,
I said, waiter, can we have the bill.

**

Found me jogging in the park.
Followed me for hours and miles, miles, miles, miles.
I tripped and almost broke my neck.
She propped me up and gave it a kiss.
And I said:

[Chorus]
Down, Vicki, down
Down, down, Vicki, down, down, down, down.
I don't want you / I don't need you.
Down, down, Vicki, down
[repeat chorus]

[Bridge]
She walks like an angel floating on air.
Talks like an aria.
She has hair like a golden halo of flowers.
Eyes like wondrous stars.
Vicki!

*

[guitar segue]

I don't know what to do.
She turns my world upside down.
I think I'm losing my mind.
I don't know who you are,
Vicki!

*

[guitar solo]

Down, Vicki, down.
Vicki.
Down, down, Vicki, down, down, down, down.
I don't want you / I don't need you
Down, down, Vicki, down.
[repeat chorus]

**

[spoken]
Oh, down, Vicki,
Yeah Vicki,
Oh Vicki, that feels real good!

***

17/Jun/2005

Songs: Coming home

Home is my lifeline

[piano accompaniment]

If I could find my way back home
I wouldn't waste my time away
Travelling over starry shores
If only I could find my way back… home

Taking orders, I confess
I search my mind for some success
I've seen too much out on the edge
If only I could find my way back… home

[chorus]
Home is my lifeline
Home is my lifeline
Home is my lifeline
Home is my lifeline

Dreaming of my long, lost love
So faraway, but close at heart,
I lie awake at nights alone
Her heartbeats singing me the way back… home

It seems a thousand years
I left behind all trace of humankind
I see the stars where I began
my journey's almost taken me back… home

Home is my lifeline / I wanna go home
Home is my lifeline / let me go home
Home is my lifeline
Home is my lifeline

I wouldn't leave it all alone
My lifeline's calling me back home
If only I could find my way
If only I don't go insane

Home is my lifeline
Home is my lifeline [x3]
Home is my lifeline.

***

27/Aug/2007

Songs: Crime in the city

Man With a Gun:

[Harmonica intro]
I've led a long life baby, have mercy 'pon me,
I'm headin' for the gallows, Executioner City.
Led a long life baby, have mercy 'pon me
You've known me two minutes, now I'm history….

*

[guitar intro]

[fade in]
A man with a gun
Man with a gun

**

Happened when you shot a man and left him out for dead
Because you're loaded with aggression and you're killin' on the run.
You feel no sorrow, 'coz the other man he did you wrong,
but it is no excuse to run around because you've got a gun…

*

[chorus]
A man with a gun
A scary man with a gun
Man with a gun
Lonely man with a gun

**

A gun is not a cure for anger, hate, or your depression.
And now you're momma's only son who prays you don't get shot down dead.
Drown it in the river or oblivion for you
inside the deepest darkest cell they'll throw you 'coz you've got a gun.

*

[chorus]
A man with a gun
You're no big man with a gun
Man with a gun
Little man with a gun

*

[guitar solo]

[chorus]
A man with a gun
A scary man with a gun
Man with a gun
Lonely man with a gun

**

Revenge, avenge, it doesn't matter, coz it's plainly wrong
And you will never get away with it, with blood stains on your hands.
The face of death you see at nights is not your victim's one
Because you'll find it's shiny, grey, and heavy and it's called a gun.

*

[chorus]
A man with a gun
You're no big man with a gun
Man with a gun
Little man with a gun

*

[Guitars/ drums (clash bang, clash bang) –fade out]

*

[fade in outro]
Have mercy 'pon me
Mercy 'pon me
Have mercy 'pon me
Mercy 'pon me…..[fade out]

***

Undated and uncompleted.

Been Around the World

I've been around the world before
Seen around the world before
Been all round the world
Seen all round the world

Diamonds, roses, limousines
can't compare with what you're seen
I've even dined with kings and queens

I've been around the world before
Seen around the world before
Been all round the world
Seen all round the world

She's a hundred miles per hour kind of girl
Been round the world before
The world revolves beneath tanned feet
sinned round the world before

Whatcha gonna give me/What can you give me
What have you in this world?

Been around the world before
Seen around the world before
Been all round the world
Seen all round the world

***

Undated and uncompleted.

Scared

I'll be scared for you
if you love me true
I'll be scared, scared, scared.

No one wants me to fall in love with you
I'll be scared, scared, scared.

If I could fly – I'd show the world to you
If I could swim – I'd cross the furthest seas
If I could climb – I'd scale the highest highs
If I could fly, if I could fly.

I'll be scared for you
if you love me true
I'll be scared, scared, scared.

No one told me to fall in love with you
I'll be scared, scared, scared.

If I could fly – I'd show the world to you
If I could swim – I'd cross the furthest seas
If I could climb – I'd scale the highest highs

Because I love you
Because I love you
Because I love you

***

Ray TV

Introduction

I have always enjoyed writing stories and watching TV. At some point, I decided to combine my two passions and start creating TV shows of my own; things I would like to watch. Some ideas were better than others and while I can't remember the impetus which led me to start sending my ideas to production companies, in 2005, I started sending TV programme proposals to various production studios. I also would post the ideas back to myself in recorded mail with the envelope seal signed by myself and taped over – a supposed lazy-man's copyright.

There were a lot of rejections, but some good advice, like with Eagle & Eagle TV – to have any success of attracting a commissioner my proposals would have to promise something new and unique in the way of story or access. TV is a very competitive business, and you have to offer something special that others don't have or have not thought of before.

Over the years, my endeavours certainly led to some interesting doors being open both for experience and in creative ways.

The TV shows presented below are all my creations and presented in their original form or where noted updated as my style of presentation changed, hopefully for the better. I offer views into some of the shows' inception and other tidbits to delve into.

In some cases, I note when and where I had submitted my ideas to and the feedback I received.

Original 04/Jul/2005 updated 29/Nov/2007

Comic Book Weekly

2020 vision

I sent this idea to **Five**, July 2005, but got rejected. I also sent it to **Talent TV** and later to **Illuminations Media** both in April 2006. The feedback from the latter is that they developed their own ideas internally.

Examining the popularity of comic books and heroes in the modern age. I had been collecting comic books since 1985 (starting with DC's Star Trek comic #18) until around 2007 when I started selling them off to scrounge for money while I was unemployed. Anyway, I've always thought there should be a TV show about comic books even before the proliferation of comic book films, exploring the mythology and history of comic books and superheroes. I think we can still do with one now...

Premise: Examining the enduring popularity of the comic book on world culture.

Introduction :

'Why do superheroes matter in this day and age? Do they? Are they modern-day equivalents to the old gods or heroes of the future? Do they represent something within ourselves today? **Comic Book Weekly** will take a timely, if somewhat irreverent peek into the world of the superheroes.'

Structure :

This half-hour programme will delve into comic books and spin-off graphic novels, films, television shows, merchandising, books, conventions, computer games and many more incarnations of comic book heroes via interviews, shop visits, emails, competitions, etc. This original programme will be successful because it deals exclusively with this genre, while other shows (e.g. news clips, film specials, etc) focus on it short-term when a comic book becomes a film adaptation. **Comic Book Weekly** will be a constant and accessible source of information without resorting to repeated satellite shows, the Internet or quickly out-of-date magazines.

The people behind the scenes: writers, artists, inkers, letterers, et al and the actors who breathe life into these heroes will also be featured. The Legends' Corner will recall writers and artists from the past who contributed to the wealth of the genre. The works of DC Comics, Image, Homage, Marvel, 2000 AD and others will reveal what it takes to be successful and how to create and perpetuate enduring characters. Competitions could also be held to find and/or appreciate new writers and artists.

The impact of superhero television series, both live and animated, has boosted the aura of the comic book world, even though the comic book itself was in decline. The rise of women and minority comic book characters are on the increase with an Indian version of Spider-Man and a Middle Eastern super-group planned. Light-hearted discussions with anthropologists and psychologists could also analyse the superhero 'psyche' and worldwide fandom phenomena.

Meanwhile…

With the popularity of *Heroes*, the Batman, Superman and Spider-Man films, **Comic Book Weekly** will appeal to adults, who clog the comic books shops buying for themselves and their children, and also to children who love comic books and want to experience alternative reading and entertainment. This programme represents the chance to be both enthralled by the heroics of superheroes and also to look within ourselves and see those heroes reflected back.

End.

27/Nov/2005

The Dominican Republic – Tourism's Killing the Archaeology

2020 vision
This unfinished show was thought of after learning about it in a class at university. It was to be the start of a documentary series called 'Hidden World' about archaeological sites being destroyed for commerce and tourism. While this show was not fleshed out, the follow up 'Hidden London' is presented further below. It also formed part of 'Archaeology Nightmares', March 2009.

Premise: An investigative report into the wilful destruction of archaeology to build hotels and tourism trade.

Introduction:
Billionaire playboys, their private airport, hotel chain and the faking of white beaches with processed limestone. The destruction of native mangroves for foreign coconut trees and goats. They are legitimised by Harvard academics for their ecologically sustainable programme, while the archaeology is destroyed, looted or under managed looked after by corrupt officials.

17/Jan/2006

Mars – Are We There Yet?

2020 vision

I have a passion for Mars and belive we will have a human on Mars in my lifetime. I have been a member of the Mars Society for almost 20 years. While a mission to Mars has been discussed endlessly and shown in films, when the real mission arrives, how will we keep the public's interest alive on a 7 to 9-month mission? This was a show to start that interest off and build momentum until we had boots on Martian soil.

I had sent in this idea to **Pioneer Productions** in January 2006 and while the contact was impressed with my initiative and asked me to call him, I don't have further details of the call we had or contact after that so nothing came of the idea.

Premise: An updated programme on Man's readiness for a mission to the Red Planet.

We have been going to Mars for the last thirty years, but are we there yet? With ESA forging ahead with Aurora and NASA gearing up for Moon-Mars missions, have we finally come to a consensus for going to Mars? What will it take in human, financial and other costs? Who will have the courage to take us there, whether political, corporate, private or public interests? Mars: Are we there yet?

The focus of this bold programme will be on the reality of a manned exploration of Mars. There will be professional opinions from and interview with scientists, astronauts, engineers, space writers and other professionals.

Views from NASA, ESA, Roskosmos, the Chinese, and other international space agencies will be sought, the alliances of shifting politics, space missions, current work and visions of the future discussed. National space institutions can be contrasted to private enterprises like the Mars Society, Scaled Composites-Virgin Galactic, Xcor and Armadillo Aerospace, etc, who are spearheading a private movement for manned space exploration. With the addition of the billionaire 'thrillionaires', 'space tourists', and celebrity sponsors, will they use their private resources to fund future space missions further afield than Earth orbit? Will they stoke public awareness and allay fears of wasted public money?

Science fiction vs. science fact, humans versus robot exploration, cost versus practicality are some issues to be resolved. Are there any trickle-back technologies and benefits? What are the near-term costs: Monetary, technological and human life?

And what will we do when we get to Mars? Explore, study, mine for resources, terraform; stay for long term, short term and then leave?

Mars exploration is an issue as relevant as any current topic that deals with our future. Are we ready to go? What are the long-term costs: Political, economic, cultural, biological and moral implications to the human race on Mars? Do we know what we want to do? Are we there yet?

End.

02/Mar/2006

Par For The Course

2020 vision
An unfinished comedy idea. And I don't even like golf!

Premise: 'Everyone Loves Raymond' meets the golf course.

Introduction: A British 'Ray Romano'-type, newly retired, desires to play the perfect game of golf. Interrupting his dream are his family, dominating wife, meddlesome-yet-over-loving mother, zany brother-in-law and (unspecified) children.

Episodes: Prone to dreaming before his big day, they seem to come true one way or another. For instance. The man and his brother-in-law are playing on a new course and come across a fence that his ball has gone over. The sign says 'driving range', but is muddy and pockmarked. Two boards form steps over the fence. The man sees his chance to go for the ball. However as he steps toward the middle of the range, tanks come flying over the ridge, shells flying, bombs going off and mines exploding. Ducking for cover, the man gestures to his brother-in-law for help. The brother gets the two boards ready to climb over but notices something written on them. One says 'Army', the other says 'keep out'. Holding the boards up to the other sign he sees 'Army Driving range. Keep out.' He shrugs and watches helplessly as the tanks race by, smoke obscuring his brother. When the tanks are gone, his brother comes out from a hiding place behind a tree. A bit dishevelled, he clambers over the fence. Another day wasted.

His biggest nightmare comes true as his mother makes a bid to become a golfer to be closer to him. Ultimately, he is his own worst enemy, prone to 'Frasier' moments of self-doubt, guilt and over-confidence.

Will he ever have the perfect game of golf?

End.

03/Nov/2006

Scientific Today

2020 vision
Proposal sent into the **BBC** July 2005, but rejected, with the same advice regarding accepting unsolicited material from the same Proposals Assistant. Though the idea was also rejected by **Five** as not quite fitting their current brief they did invite me to send in more ideas which were more appropriate for Science at **Five**. I had also sent in this idea to **Pioneer Productions** in January 2006, **Talent TV** in April 2006, and **Maverick TV** in June 2006.

Premise: 'Tomorrow's World' meets 'The Wright Stuff'!

Introduction:
Science and technology are a part of everyone's lives, but few have the chance to delight in inquisitive thinking or to experience its inventive process. A new prime-time science and technology programme is needed to recapture the genius of inventiveness, highlighting Britain's role in science and asking mind-expanding questions.

This exciting, one-hour, weekly and interactive programme will bring together those above elements. Terrestrial television is bereft of straight programmes revelling in the wonder of technology and science. With one recent exception (Five's *'The Gadget Show'*) most shows look to the past and wonder what past cultures did for us (*'What the (insert culture name) did for us'* series –BBC2), or are dressed up as engineering fun (*'Scrapheap Challenge'* –Channel 4 and *'Robot Wars'*), or survival challenges (*'Rough Science'* –BBC2). The yearly *'Royal Institution Christmas Lectures'* are an ideal combination of down-to-earth presentation, informative demonstration and lively audience participation, which inspires children.

Satellite channels are filling the science gap (e.g. Discovery Science Channel and 'New Scientist Reports' on Discovery Channel UK). Magazines (e.g. *Nature, New Scientist, Scientific American*, etc) have first-class articles, which are sporadically scavenged by newspapers or used as fluff or folly stories by TV news, which are then lost in the daily haze of news. **Scientific Today** will present to a wider audience a new and interactive format.

There are question shows *('Question Time', 'Test the Nation'*, etc), Talk shows *('The Wright Stuff', 'Trisha Goddard',* etc) and Info-tainment shows *('Balderdash and Piffle', 'Quite Interesting',* etc) that ask political, topical or humorous questions, but do not instil a deep thoughtfulness or promote science. **Scientific Today** would provide that challenge.

Structure:
The (co-)host(s), preferably with some scientific grounding, will guide the viewer through a selection of topics. At the heart of the programme would be a question, answered at the end of the programme. Where **Scientific Today** departs from other science/technology shows is that a 'science panel' of three scientists/inventors and another panel from the public give their opinions on the presented inventions (ala '*Dragons' Den*'), gaining instant feedback on them. This combination of expert and layperson interactivity would create moments of good-natured frisson as they use, demonstrate and debate the merits of the invention/ application. There will also be interviews and viewers' comments and emails (for details, see page 3).

Technology is sometimes criticised or viewed with suspicion, because of its remoteness, rapid pace of change, and moral implications. Science is viewed as the domain of middle-aged, bearded white men. **Scientific Today** would bring technological change into perspective and also showcase youthful, ethnic and gender-balanced views. **Scientific Today** would be a programme to make one ponder the unfathomable, the offbeat or the controversial, to challenge the think-tank that is Britain.

Scientific Today will be well-placed in the television market, appealing to core audiences of professionals, budding science students and children, enthusiasts, discerning viewers looking for educational and challenging television and those wanting the interactive component to voice their views on the subject.

Scientific Today Programme Structure

1) Introduction: 'Hello and welcome to Scientific Today, the show that brings science and technology to you and asks those all-important questions.'

2) Question Asked: The experts get to think over their answers during the programme. The questions would be from experts of varying fields, programme sources or, more importantly, the public (e.g. Is genetic modification really necessary for the human race? Is there such a thing as the religion of science or the science of religion and can they be reconciled? If you had a law, what would it be? etc).

3) The Panels: The two panels are then introduced. The experts' (from above) and public panels (from audience) view three or four quick presentations on newly invented technologies or applications. The panels give their views and opinions.

4) Ask the expert: The How-do-they-do-that section. Experts answer public questions about science and technology.

5) Book Review: Selected top ten and new science books and events.

6) Question reminder: Experts have last five minutes to ponder the question. While this happens...

7) Scientist Interview: Quick 5-minute interview with 'guest' scientist. Basic questions include: 'What they do?', 'How they got started in science?', 'What is their greatest scientific achievement? And 'What is in the future for them?'

8) Question answered (possible debate).

9) Recap and goodbye.

End.

25/Apr/2006

Hidden London

2020 vision
This was a project for friend and archaeologist, Jenny Stripe. It was basically based on her course at the Institute of Archaeology, UCL – travelling around London with students and discovering the history that is hidden by and under our modern city.

I sent to **Illuminations Media** in April 2006. The feedback from them is that they developed their own ideas internally. In October 2006 I sent this into the **BBC** who thought it was an interesting idea, but not for them and of course not from an independent production company. The assistant did suggest I try the Pact Organisation to find an independent production company to work through. **ITV** thought the idea was 'entertaining and informative' but it wasn't for them.

Premise: Archaeological tours of the hidden architecture of Roman and Medieval London.

Introduction:
This exciting, multi-part, weekly 1/2 hourly documentary series reveals parts of Roman and Medieval London hitherto unseen by the millions of Londoners and visitors who frequent museums and other sightseeing tours. Businesses, shops, public places and other parts of London stand on or obscure preserved ruins, which are inaccessible or overlooked.

The Presenter:
The proposed presenter for **Hidden London** is Jenny Stripe (MA) lecturer of *Archaeology in London: London Before the Great Fire of 1666* (Institute of Archaeology, University College London). An expert in this field, Jenny is down-to-earth and demonstrably informative. She is also dedicated and uniquely positioned to present a fresh look at our Capital's past, appealing not only to a youthful audience, but also to those enthusiastic about history and London.

Structure:
For each show, Jenny, will take the viewer on a chronological tour of London and its past. Virtual reconstructions of the hidden gems standing within modern London would show their location, surviving features and their contrasting scales and styles to the modern city. Their history, function, abandonment/destruction phases will also be discussed. Also, examined would be how archaeologists are preserving these structures and compare them to the modern building growth of present-day London.

Original programming, such as **Hidden London** would be well placed in the market of historical/archaeological programmes, with Jenny giving a valuable insight into the surprising amount of extant ruins from the past; a tantalising past that could soon disappear, hidden away.

Alternate Presenters/Structure:
Hidden London could form part of an expanded new format archaeological series, called **Hidden World,** with seasoned presenters travelling the world, with archaeological consultants finding archaeological sites that are disappearing or reappearing due to modern development, environmental change or technical/human explorations. Unlike other archaeological programmes **Hidden World** would be more of an exposé/documentary type show, rather than a search-and-excavate exercise.

As a new and exciting globetrotting archaeological series, **Hidden World**, would present to viewers a new dimension to archaeology in countries seldom known for their archaeology. **Hidden World** will witness the past as never seen before.

End.

10/Dec/2007

21st Century Vision

2020 vision

This was also an article featured on the writing site. I'm not sure how this would have worked as a TV show, but it ties into my perception that heroes and personalities - real leaders - are mising in today's society, which now worships celebrities for celebrity sake. Hopefully, people like the ones below would inspire others.

Premise: Who are the people or organisations that are already leading the way in this youthful century?

Introduction: They are not just politicians, entrepreneurs, scientists and beneficial organisations, these people are setting new agendas for the future and for a safer and enlightened world. How did they overcome 20th century paradigms to envision a different future, one that they can help come true? New ideas, new concepts and new disruptive/radical agendas are driving through these new 21st century visions.

Structure:
Every week, this narrated documentary series focuses on a person or company that is at the heart of new century thinking.

Subjects could include:
Al Gore: The global face of Climate Change awareness.
Richard Branson: Business tycoon, adventurer, Co-sponsor of the Elders.
Craig Venter: Biologist on the threshold of creating synthetic organisms that create synthetic fuels and carbon scrubbers.
Burt Rutan: Architect behind Spaceship One, the first privately owned spacecraft to enter space.
Robert Zubrin: President of the Mars Society, a group that advocates missions to and colonisation of Mars.
The Elders: The formation of a new independent political force went almost unnoticed in 2007, yet they could be the prelude to a new world political movement.

Bjorn Lomborg: the latter-day James Lovelock, once of the Green movement, but now apart of a wider, questioning and sceptical movement.

Ray Kurzweil: Futurist who envisions the synthesis of human and machine to create the Singularity.

The Global Crop Diversity Trust: Cary Fowler, the executive director of the Trust and the Norwegian Government have set up the Arctic seed vault on the Svalbard Islands. The seed bank has been built to safeguard the crop diversity in the event of a global catastrophe.

These are the latter-day Bill Gates, Steve Jobs, James Lovelock, Albert Einstein, Carl Sagan, Richard Feynman, John Kennedy and Gene Roddenberry; individuals with the vision and drive to succeed which has firmly implanted their brands into this century . Likewise Google, Amazon, PayPal and Ebay and other e-companies are the face of the internet, but what is around the corner? Is there anything that will take over and drive the 21st century vision?

End.

10/Dec/2007

The Invisible Brand

Premise: Why is there a standard look to the world and culture?

Introduction:
The quirks of branding have pervaded our world to the point where we do not recognise some of the brands that are worldwide in nature and all around us. What makes one brand better than another, especially when other products are available?

Structure:
The programme will investigate how some of our invisible technological brands came about. For instance, why are all keyboards of the 'QWERTY' variety? What is it's evolution? Also the Helvetica font and its ubiquitous presence; why is it used everywhere? Calculator number layouts also apply. Think of Ford's Edsel, a spectacular failure, but revolutionary in some respects. Why did it fail when the Ford brand was a strong marketing tool? There are mobiles, iPods and other techno-wonders that are better than others, yet the same few brands prevail against other well-known brands. The VHS vs Betamax wars, DAT tapes vs cassette tapes vs CDs vs vinyl; there are forces at work, which determine what we like and buy, but what are they.

Are we magpies and copycats, liking bright new techno-wonders and having to have what our neighbour has? How do companies research our preferences, is there subliminal messaging or are we hard-wired with certain tendencies to want certain items.

Can urban anthropologists decipher our wants and needs? Could they investigate the undercurrent of the invisible brands and discover why certain brands do better than others when there is no difference. Then there is the tale of the big green button on Xerox machines, devised by urban anthropologists; does humanity have an innate ability to produce technological brands that appeals to the quintessential soul of us all? Do we all view such technology and branding as the same (nature) or do we see it from a cultural perspective (nurture).

The Invisible Brand will take us around the world to look at human culture and their take on the branded world around them and what they understand about it.

End.

04/Jul/2005 Updated 07/Jan/2008

Crisis Climate

2020 vision
I had sent this in to **Channel 4** in July 2005. Following advice from Channel 4, I registered for their online proposal system as an individual. The **BBC** rejected the idea in September 2005, replying that while they had forwarded it to their current affairs development team for ideas, they were already planning to cover the topic in their schedule. The BBC also advised me that they didn't take unsolicited submissions, only from their own production department or from Independent Production companies. **Five** also rejected a revamped version in November 2007 as did ***Mentorn TV***, and **Pioneer Productions** in January 2008.

I still think a weekly look into the science and response to climate change would be a great eye-opener to what is happening around us, to travel to places not generally seen in the news which are acutely affected, and to hear peoples' views on it. We shouldn't have to bang people's heads over this, but provide informative and creative debate and evidence as to the reality of climate change.

Premise: 'Newsnight' meets Climate Change.

Introduction:
'Hello and welcome to **Crisis Climate**, the show that brings you up to date concerning the issues behind Global Warming. With me will be politicians, scientists, economists, environmentalists, and other commentators to discuss climate change issues and what can be done to help our world.'

Crisis Climate is a bold, new ongoing series for our times. Climate Change is an issue hotly debate within the media and in public, but facts, half-truths, statistics, second-hand information and hype are bandied about without context and in-depth analysis. **Crisis Climate** would present the issues that matter to the viewers, from first-hand leading sources and experts that other media (TV news, science magazines, newspapers, etc) could not match nor offer in scope or in viewing figures.

Structure

Every week, the presenter, possibly a news personality, will moderate panel proceedings over the half-hour, through interviews, special reports and discussions. Topics would include climate change news, local reports and other developments from the week. Questions for the panel will be taken from the public.

Some Crisis Climate Topics:

What is Climate Change? What is Global Warming? How do they differ and affect the world we live in? Is it a natural or cultural phenomenon?
What agreements have been negotiated and can they and their successors be successful? What is the Carbon Tax? Are there alternatives?
How would Global Warming affect Britain? Benefits and disadvantages?
Is it better to fight Global Warming or adapt to it?
Can technology overcome Global Warming (e.g. solar power, wind farms, nuclear and wave power, bio-fuels, carbon sequestration, congestion charging, etc)? Each technology will be examined fully in dedicated programmes.
What is the hydrogen economy? Will Iceland and California become the first hydrogen economies? Is hydrogen actually safer?
Are oil companies the big bad wolf and our saviours?
Attitudes toward Climate Change. Reports from Europe, America, Australia, Africa and other Third World countries, China, Russia, India, Brazil, etc.
Other political, economic, socio-cultural issues.
The role of the media in hyping or over-stating cases.

Crisis Climate will be a highly relevant programme offering honest, interactive, topical, and long-term debate without being preachy or pandering to hype. This issue will not go away and every week will inform viewers about what is happening around the world, and what we can do to help us all.

End.

07/Jan/2008

The Sceptics Advocate

2020 vision
This idea was sent to ***Mentorn TV*** 07.01.08 and then to ***Five*** on 19.02.09, who rejected it for their 10pm slot. I had some great advice from a producer at ***Five*** in my request for work advice: I didn't need an academic background or a 'Mickey Mouse' degree in media, just lots of determination, be pushy, and proactive. Write to 20 production companies and start from the bottom as a runner or in research. Get my ideas noticed as TV companies live and die by ideas. I kept that in mind and kept going.

Premise: TV for sceptics by sceptics.

Introduction:
The Sceptics Advocate is a bold and provocative new series for our times. There is a perceived notion by the public that TV news programmes cannot be fully trusted because of bias and spin via politics or other controlling authorities. Many news programmes do not ask questions or bring up subjects that may offend the establishment or their core audience, so people are sceptical of the news, because they do not see the 'official events' as truly reflecting within their worldview. **The Sceptics Advocate** redresses this balance by having the public set the agenda for this programme. With people seeking their news on the internet or other alternate sources, **the Sceptics Advocate** would also bring back viewership from those other sources.

Structure:
Every week, the news presenter, possibly an 'anti-establishment' figure, will moderate proceedings over the hour, acting as a devil's advocate on subjects through reports, interviews and debates. The public can write in, video or email their ideas for stories, and have a right of reply forum against TV and newspapers, whether from the fringe, controversial topics or even conspiracy theories.

Topics could include:

Why do some media outlets show a perceived bias? Who controls the media and what do they gain from their subjective broadcasts?

So what if the Iraq war was about oil? Everybody uses it in its different forms.

Why shouldn't Iran have nuclear weapons? It would balance world order.

Should we really have to do anything about Climate Change? We could adapt.

It doesn't matter if America doesn't sign up to Kyoto. When America does act, they will be at the forefront, because of the enormous financial gains.

Why not negotiate with terrorists and dictators? They act on fear and force, but diplomacy is the (disarming) art of not being afraid to talk.

Would it really have mattered if Diana was pregnant with Dodi's baby? What threat could a Muslim baby related to the Royal family have posed?

Who are the Elders and is this a prelude to a revolution in world government? Israel/Palestine: A homeland model for the Kurds?

Was Ted Kaczynski (the Unabomber) right about technological progress? How can humans be saved from being slaves to technology?

Despite the title and topic ranges, **The Sceptics Advocate** is not a rant for free speech, nor panders to conspiracy theorists or political agendas. It offers an alternative approach to news reporting and measured debate about stories that often remain hidden behind other stories or not reported on at all. The public want more than a news desk reporter with repeating news, they want to know what else they may not be hearing, they want fresh perspectives, reassurance that their views are aired, they want news with their questions answered. **The Sceptics Advocate** would answer that call.

End.

20/Nov/2008

Jump The Shark

Premise: Panel game show celebrating the over-the-top moments from TV and news.

Introduction:
Jump the Shark refers to the phrase 'Jumping the Shark' which was first used in reference to the *Happy Days* episode where Fonzie jumped over a shark on water skis. It denotes a TV show in decline which uses drastic plots or characters to revive a show. There are many instances of this such as in *My Hero* replacing the lead actor for the same character, or *Dynasty*'s UFO episode or Bo and Luke Duke from *The Dukes of Hazzard* being replaced by look-alike cousins Coy and Vance, etc.

But Jumping the Shark can also refer to the Political or Entertainment world, with Tom Cruise jumping on Oprah's couch, Britney Spears cutting off her hair, or George W. Bush with his 'Mission Accomplished' sign.

Jump the Shark will celebrate the inventiveness(?) or lack thereof and the loveable absurdity of TV and the over-the-top hyperbole of politics and entertainment from another perspective.

Structure:
Every week on the half-hour show, the two three-person panels, hosted by a moderator will be given a series of Jump the Shark challenges:

The 'what happened next' segment starts the game, where the panels have to decide what the Jump the Shark moment is that comes after a TV show or news clip is presented (e.g. *Dallas*' Bobby Ewing emerging from the shower after his 'death' the previous season). Points are awarded to the correct or funniest suggestion.

The Multiple choice section includes the 'which Jump the Shark' moment did a particular TV show employ (e.g. Replacement actor, new location, new baby, etc). Points awarded for correct answer with bonus for other factual info about the change.

The Panels have to create Jump the Shark scenes for TV shows (e.g. Phil and Grant Mitchell from *Eastenders* discover that they have a black brother, with hilarious consequences!) or what a politician will do next.

The last quick-fire quiz round quizzes the panellists on a host of Jump the Shark facts or fallacies from around the world. This would include True or False questions, hidden words from written descriptions of Jump the Shark moments, and pictures of actors/politicians who acted/enacted those Jump the Shark scenes. Most points wins.

Jump the Shark will also offer viewers a chance to see and analyse with hindsight and humour when/where things went wrong for the TV shows, politicians, and entertainers after their Jump the Shark moment.

End.

07/Feb/2009

KIDS RULE

2020 vision
This was sent to **Five** as an idea, but rejected.

Premise: The 'Wright Stuff' for kids by kids.

Introduction:
Kids Rule is a bold and fun new series for 7 to 16 year olds. Kids have their own views on the world and we should hear from them and not what adults think kids should think. Politicians do not get this and pander to authorities and condescend to kids. We need to reflect a kid's worldview where adults can learn from kids.

Kids Rule redresses this balance by having young people set the agenda for this programme and let kids tell us what they want, how they feel, and what they need in their own words.

Structure:
Every week, the presenters, a boy and a girl in their early to mid-teens, will moderate proceedings over the half-hour, debating kid's issues, conducting interviews, and answering questions (from emails, phone-ins, and studio audience). Having a 'Wright Stuff' type panel of peers would help children to address their issues without the fear of adult reproach or misunderstanding. The audience could be visiting classrooms ala 'The Christmas Lecture' series, where audience interaction is encouraged.

Kids Rule would let the kids speak for themselves; free to debate without psychoanalysts studying their every word. Children are used for humour in Saturday matinee shows or just in special one-off news reports, but **Kids Rule** would be a more serious and long-term prospect. Test shows could be premiered during half-term or summer holidays following Five's children's programming to assess audience levels.

Issues:
What do children think of: Bullying, sex, drugs, alcohol, crime, celebrity, politics, mobiles phones & internet, social networking, single parent

families, divorce, adoption, race issues, health and safety over sports and school trips, school dinners, corporal punishment, learning difficulties, problem children, apprenticeships and higher education, being a child star or prodigy, being rich or poor, and climate change? What do kids want to learn? What do kids make of using kids in social experiments like '*Supernanny*', any Professor Robert Winston series, or '*Kids Alone*'? Children have no external input into these shows, but **Kids Rule** will be precisely for that.

These issues could be collected from a kid's look through the newspapers. Lastly, kids can ask: what rules would they make for themselves –The Kids Commandments?

Summary:
Kids Rule offers an alternative approach to news reporting and measured debate about stories that adults often think children do not understand or care about. Kids want fresh perspectives, reassurance that their views are aired, and they want shows with their questions answered. **Kids Rule** would answer that call.

End.

17/Feb/2009

WEB TV

2020 vision
This was sent to **Five**, but rejected, mostly as it would be difficult to pull off as good entertaining TV and my proposal did not overcome this.

Premise: A TV 'book club' for websites

Introduction:
Everyday, millions of people use the internet for business, entertainment, or research, whether for international, national, local or personal purposes. But the World Wide Web is growing exponentially and there is no time to search through and make sense of it all beyond the big brand name offerings.

In Brief:
Web TV is an irreverent, half-hour, light entertainment programme dedicated to websites. Websites are usually only featured on TV within brief news reports about companies, other consumer programmes, or video funnies; while TV shows now feature on the internet. **Web TV** will showcase in more detail those 'weird and wonderful' websites that would be of interest for anyone from aged 8 to 80 -in short, an informal and breezy jape through the bizarre world of the web. **Web TV** is not a 'video funnies' or a 'which website' comparison show, but one that can act as a semi-directory to the ins and outs of finding those out-of-the-way gems.

Structure:
Web TV's two web-savvy presenters will direct proceedings with humourous candour, without 'techno-babble'. Video and websites can be shown on big, touch-screen TVs (a la Channel 4 news) for presentation purposes. There is no studio audience.

Interviews will consist of informal in-studio or online interviews. The website name/URL, name of person/company running site (with permission), brief description of site, its purpose, and other details, would be discussed. Any subject (e.g. novelty/niche, new sites, fan groups, etc) of a particular site can be covered depending upon vetting of the site's content, subject to time availability of the programme, and suitability for TV viewing. Other topics covered could include trends, fads, cons/threats, and successes, and bring recognition to deserving sites beyond the SEO reach. Due to the nature of the programme it is suitable to show at any time, especially in the 19.30 slot, as it would be attractive to a wide demographic audience. And of course, segments of or the whole show would feature on TV or the web.

Celebrity endorsements of their favourite sites, new technologies, and the future of the web could be examined. Advertisement breaks could feature more businesses with websites, with tie-ins and links to and from the TV show (e.g. 'as featured in **Web TV**'), thereby adding more revenue to **FIVE** as more clientele vie to be included in this unique forum that will showcase them to an otherwise unaware nation.

Web TV, the future of the web on TV.

End.

WINDFALL FILMS

On 04.03.09, the UCL Alumni Relations held a Professional Networking Event for PR, Journalism, and Broadcasting at the London Television Centre, London. One of the guest speakers was David Dugan, the Company Chairman from independent production company Windfall Films. After the talks, many of us crowded around him asking questions and getting advice. I got his card and the next day I started sending him TV show ideas.

After several months, my efforts finally paid off and after a friendly meeting in September at Channel 4, where he and a colleague had finished a meeting, we discussed my work and future. It went well. I started a two-week work shadow experience at Windfall Films in October from 19th to 28th, under David Dugan and the then Head of Development, Emily Roe. I created prospective TV programmes, researched ideas for further programmes, and developed contacts for said programmes. I had hoped to maintain contacts after and to either work at Windfall Films or continue to send in TV programme ideas for future work.

After being unemployed for a while in 2007-2008, I was now working as a concierge. I attended Windfall Films between shifts or took annual leave. At first I had expected to be paid, but it turned out as that as I wasn't a current student from UCL, I didn't qualify for the payments, which was extremely disappointing.

So at the time I had absolutely no money as my concierge earnings were stretched to the limit. I was lunching on flapjacks and sunflowers seeds with ribena juice boxes. I never socialised with the staff members when they invited me each day out to lunch as I was too embarrassed to admit I had no money. Plus, as a newcomer, I was a bit quiet and just got on with my work, asking questions and taking research advice as needed. Even though David and I had discussed being hired while we talked in the boardroom, in the end I believe my perceived introvertness scuppered my chances of being hired; not good, especially in an industry which thrives on contacts and relationships. But despite this, I'm grateful I got the experience.

Although I was not employed by them we kept in touch for a while with the possibility of a few weeks of work in December and further projects as far as April 2010 then as my sci-fi novel writing took over and work duties grew, the emails stopped between us. Maybe I could have been a bit more ambitious and 'pushy' but, just as with my article writing, it seemed the right time to lay that to rest and move on. But I still had a few ideas after and every now and again, I jot down a new idea.

Below are some of the efforts I sent to them or created while at their offices.

07/Mar/2009

Archaeology Nightmares

2020 vision
This was one of the first ideas sent into Windfall Films along with Celebrity Archaeology and Underground Press.

Premise: What is the stuff of an Archaeologist's nightmare?

Introduction:
Archaeology has been televised in its varied form from the placid, time-honoured 'Time Team' model, rescue archaeology, aerial archaeology, underwater archaeology, extreme archaeology, and heritage studies. These Programmes cover such diverse locations stretching from Britain to Egypt to Lost Cities.

We see unflappable archaeologists and historians busily working away, but what do they fear the most about their business? What can go wrong? Can historical sites be saved from destruction? **Archaeology Nightmares** reveals those things that could see everything archaeologists work for destroyed.

Programme structure:
The narrator and 'talking heads' from the world of archaeology talk us through their nightmare scenarios in this one-off special programme.

1. Tourism:
Archaeological sites can draw in the tourists, but too much development and tourism can actually destroy the sites they have come to marvel. Under threat: Peru - the Inca Trail and Machu Picchu under threat from too many trekkers. The Dominican Republic - billionaire businessmen are constructing a luxury compound, building fake white-sand beaches, and destroying archaeology along the way. The Giza Pyramids - interiors protected from condensation left by tourists' humid visits. And Babylon bears the indignity of Saddam imprinted bricks. Too much tourism could cause irreparable damage not only to building fabrics, but also to the environment.

2. War:
Besides sites located within or close to military enclosures and territory (Egyptian Pyramids, Iraqi Ziggurats, Stonehenge on Salisbury Plain), no one contemplated the destruction of archaeological wonders until 2001 and the Taliban's destruction of the Buddhas of Bamyan. This was war against culture. In Sudan, archaeologists work, while hundreds of miles away war rages. In Uganda or Bosnia, archaeologists could be suborned as a forensics officer to find or identity victims of war. Various countries erupt into seemingly spontaneous riots (Uzbekistan, Peru, Bolivia), which could see an archaeologist placed in harms way. But the work must go on, lest sites are destroyed in anger and lost forever.

3. Credit Crunch
Credit Crunch archaeology has been around for a long time. It encompasses loss of funding for excavation, loss of jobs, site disrepair, looting for money, metal detecting Nighthawks, and black market antiquities dealers, and fakers. Archaeology is not the search for treasure, not in the material sense; the richness comes from completing another story of mankind's life. When our past is lost due to modern financial troubles and moral dilemmas, we all become the poorer for it.

4. Climate Change
The future of archaeology will change as sites are exposed, eroded, flooded, or abandoned as climate and the environment changes. The past may be sacrificed to save the present and future. Will the far north and far south yield new sites as temperate regions become uninhabitable? Will old sites be looted for materials and resources for survival? Now, more than ever, the archaeologist will have to contend with a changing landscape much as our ancestors did.

<u>Audience draw</u>:
Archaeologists have found only a fraction of a percent of the artefacts left by previous civilisations and cultures. And it is disappearing at an increasing rate as humans and natural factors conspire to endanger or obliterate sites from history. How much of our human heritage can be saved and preserved for future generations?

Archaeology Nightmares: Saving the past despite the fear of loss.

End.

07/March/2009

Celebrity Archaeology

2020 vision
This idea was liked with celebrites literally digging up their ancient past having appeal, but then thoughts turned to the insurance for celebrities and the expectation of them spending several weeks training. Compared to celebrity reality shows nowadays this wouldn't have been such a big deal.

Premise: 'Who Do You Think You Are?' meets 'Time Team'.

Introduction:
The trend of tracing the background of celebrities breaks new ground in allowing celebrities to help excavate in their 'ancestral' lands to discover more about themselves and the journey their ancestors took.

Programme structure:
Train. Dig. Experience.
Various celebrities will be trained over a few weeks in the basics of general archaeology, a specialist function, and the cultural background of the region they are going to work in. Willing archaeology companies will then employ and whisk the volunteer celebrity teams away to live and work alongside trained archaeologists. The length of the dig will depend on company funding and contracts. Work can consist of field work, finds sorting, geoarchaeology, lab work, post-excavation, and more.

The celebrities will choose sites from their cultural/genetic background and should have a passion for learning about themselves and their distant past. Here, they can place themselves in the context of living hundreds or thousands of years ago, touching artefacts their ancestral society made, and maybe even digging up an ancestor or two. Imagine the celebrity hold the bone of someone who could be their ancestor from thousands of years ago. This experience will take them far beyond paper history and genealogy.

At the end of the excavation, the celebrities will contribute a written essay either for a future publication and/or for the final site report.

Audience draw:
Celebrity Archaeology would be for those viewers who do not care for celebrities who appear on reality TV for seemingly no reason (though charity money is raised) or for those who cannot get enough of ubiquitous celebrity reality shows. In **Celebrity Archaeology**, the newly recruited celebrity archaeologists will be working to an end, personally working to uncover their own past, participating in a cultural event that already appeals to viewers, drawing attention to the field of archaeology where people will see how the past can directly affect the digger, and inspiring others to investigate their remote pasts.

The Celebrity Archaeologist will know more than just who they think they are; they will reveal their history stretching back into the depths of time.

End.

07/Mar/2009

The Underground Press

Premise: Revealing the origins of London's tube network advertising.

Introduction:
Have you ever wondered why particular ads appear more than others on the underground? How do some books get advertised and not others? Why is Jack Daniels plastered along the walls rather than on TV? Which films are targeted for the tube? Which travel agencies and destinations, job search sites, cds, TV programmes, and mobile phone deals are sent underground to woo weary passengers? **The Underground Press** will be a guide through the world of underground infotainment and how it affects us.

Programme structure:
In this one-off, one-hour programme, the history of the Tube's advertising campaign is revealed. When did advertising start? Which companies prefer such advertising over other types of Public Relations? Does it work –who has the statistics on successful tube advertising? Which companies research, design, pitch, test, supply, and maintain the advertising? What are the different types of advertising? Do the public care for the ads and how can (or do) the public decide future ad trends? The programme assesses whether advertising is better than blank walls or art-filled walls.

The programme will feature three strands interspersed through the series:
1. Following an ad campaign from start to finish (possibly an author's book)
2. Tagging along with the men and women who paste the ads and maintain them.
3. Getting behind distinctive ads (possibly Jack Daniels) and why they chose the tube?

Lastly, what is the future of underground advertising? How economical will such advertising be in the Credit Crunch years? Will digital images take the place of paper hoardings? Will ads be more targeted via Bluetooth or equivalent applications through mobiles? Will the subjects of advertising change? **The Underground Press** will be brought to the surface and people made aware of the work that goes into keeping our journeys less boring.

Audience draw:

Whether consciously or subliminally, the public are accustomed to advertising on the Underground, but have they really thought about what goes into the making of the ads, where they come from, and how they may affect their journeys? **The Underground Press** will shed new light on the advertising that flashes by as we travel throughout the day.

End.

10/Mar/2009

A Drink or Two

Premise: You make it, they drink it.

Introduction:
A Drink or Two is a liquid-inspired companion to 'Come Dine with Me', a programme that will appeal to the serious beverage connoisseur. Around the country, many passionate professionals and amateurs spend time and money creating their own perfect brews, cocktails, health drinks and other concoctions, but they do not have outlets or an appreciative forum through which to promote their products. **A Drink or Two** will remedy this by showcasing their talents and fluid inventions.

A Drink or Two will also turn the focus on drinks, as food has been in the spotlight for many years, yet the right drink can often compliment the meal and some drinks are as important as food as they are essentially liquidised food products. **A Drink or Two** will promote responsible drinking. This is not a programme about binge drinking, pub crawling, or an excuse for gratuitous indulgence, but an attempt to show the creativity, process, and business behind producing a great beverage.

Programme structure:
A Drink or Two will be divided into categories such as:

Home brewed Beers, wines, cocktails, and health drinks/juices
Little known or unappreciated British brands of beers and wines
Little known foreign brands (Asian, Eastern European, South African, etc)
Rare drinks, recreated recipes, and other oddities.

As in 'Come Dine with Me', competing strangers will meet at a fellow contestants house and make or bring their unique beverages. Amongst the conversation, tasting and testing, the contestant will explain their product and why it should be more appreciated or even on the market. The other contestants throughout the contest will vote for their favourite drink.

To add more pressure the drinks could be tested by experts or celebrity connoisseurs such as: (possibly) wine expert Oz Clarke or Jilly Goolden, actor and beer brewer Neil Morrissey, and nutritionist Amanda Hamilton or Gillian McKeith. They will put their seal of approval on the drink or sink the project. Depending on the viability and availability of opportunities, the winner could be offered the chance to market their product with a professional outlet.

Audience draw:
Far from being a drunken fest, **A Drink or Two** could pique the nation's interest in the art of brewing, selecting an appropriate beverage, or promoting little-known brands. The programme will be an antidote to the binge culture and show that there are responsible ways to drink and to profit from it. So, let us celebrate another form of food and have **A Drink or Two.**

End.

12/Sept/2009

The Seven Wonders Series

2020 vision
After sending in this and a few more ideas below, I finally got the nod - Would you be able to come to meet us to discuss these ideas? Meet at Channel 4 studios - I was a little bit excited...

Premise: Experts pick the seven wonders of their respective fields.

Introduction:
Everyone knows the Seven Wonders of the Ancient World and new lists for modern Seven Wonders are always being complied. But beyond architecture and man-made places, what would experts from various fields pick as their own Seven Wonders?

Programme structure:
Each one hour programme would pose the question to a number of experts, seen making their choices (whether individually or in a group). Their choices would then be collated, described and explored. A narrator would provide the central voice and guide to each wonder.

Rather than being Top 10 or 100 lists of the biggest and best, the Seven Wonders Series would be a guide to the facts and mysteries around us. It would be a condensed lesson about our world. Some Wonders may be obvious, but other may be totally challenging, unexpected, fun, eclectic, educational, and inspirational.

Programmes could include:

The Seven Wonders of the Animal World – Strange tales of creatures and critters.
The Seven Wonders of Earth – Natural scenes of the world.
The Seven Wonders of the Seven Seas – ocean secrets, fancy fish, and hidden worlds.
The Seven Wonders of History – momentous events in history.
The Seven Wonders of Archaeology –Artefacts humans made or invented.
The Seven Wonders of the Internet – Mysteries of the web.

The Seven Wonders of Humanity – What makes us special?
The Seven Wonders of the Solar System - Tourist traps of our stellar neighbourhood.
The Seven Wonders of all time – From the Big Bang to 2009.
The Seven Wonders of the future – The Futurologists' forecast.

Audience draw:
The Seven Wonders Series is a programme of essentials. As with the seven ancient wonders, which commemorated the seven must-see, all-famous marvels of their time, what would our lives and environment boil down to if only the essentials could be chosen? If experts wanted to promote the most pertinent elements of their fields of endeavour, what would they be? And would we agree?

The Seven Wonders Series would be a fun and informative way of gleaning information about ourselves and our world in point-form video. It would encourage others to think about their essentials, create their own lists for comparison, and maybe encourage decision makers in applying such guides to our world in order to educate and preserve the wonders we see and create.

End.

12/Sept/2009

Lost Aviation Wonders of the World

Premise: Seven flying machines 'lost' in the midst of time.

Introduction:
Almost lost and forgotten are these aviation wonders, whether hanging in museums, rusting in hangers, or completely moth-balled. They could have changed the face of aviation, had they survived, with their sheer physical presence or their unique and imaginative qualities.

Programme structure:
Each week, the half-hour programmes will trace the history, development, controversy, and downfall of the specified aircraft:

1. The Hughes H-4 Hercules: The Spruce Goose (1947). The Howard HughesBehemoth everyone said would not fly until he proved them wrong. But why did it not take off commercially?

2. Avro Canada CF-105 Arrow: Canada's greatest aviation achievement (1958). How did it all go wrong for the world's most advanced aircraft of its time?

3. The XB-70 Valkyrie supersonic bomber (1964). The six-engine, supersonic bomber that never made it due to changing times and technology.

4. The Russian Ekranoplan KM: The Caspian Sea Monster (1967). The monstrous sea plane that could have changed the course of the Cold War.

5. Tupolev TU-144 (Russian Concorde) (1973). If 'Concordski' had survived as a competitive rival to Concorde, would they be more cost effective and flying today?

6. The Sikorsky S-72 X-Wing (1976). What happened to the once and future holy grail of flight, combining the helicopter and the jet aircraft?

7. The Russian Buran Space Shuttle (1988): Was this copy as superior to the NASA shuttle as claimed and how would it have affected the new space race?

Comanche stealth helicopter –standby

Audience draw:

This is a historical look at past aircraft that would have been great in their time and legends beyond had they not been killed off before their time. Some of the aircraft are well known others not so, but it is the sheer imagination, technological engineering feats and the controversial tales behind them that will serve to remind us of aviation follies or to inspire us to greater heights. Lost Aviation Wonders of the World may be lost to the air, but they are not forgotten by us.

End.

12/Sept/2009

Thrillionaire – The Billionaire Thrill Seekers
(First concept)

2020 vision
The feedback on this was great - Thanks for sending in these ideas.. 'I think the *Thrillionaire* territory is very interesting and you're obviously really keen to get something off the ground.'

Premise: Charting the rise of the adventurous billionaire seeking extreme thrills.

Introduction:
Being a Billionaire is not enough. Hostile takeovers are not de rigueur anymore. One has to show the world that they are ready to use their riches to explore all avenues of thrills, exploration, and extreme investment. This has culminated in the new commercial space race, the space tourist, and some say the death of Steve Fossett.

Beyond their claims of humanitarian endeavours, providing future space experiences for the public, and saving the space industry, are deeper concerns that this oligarchy could end up creating false dawns while putting their own lives unnecessarily under threat, in pursuit of vain-glorious passions.

Programme structure:
This one-hour, one-off programme will explore the phenomenon of the Thrillionaire by charting the rise of the millionaire explorers and adventurers from the past to the 21st century Thrillionaires of today. This would be accomplished through interviews (of the participants themselves, colleagues and friends) and archive/modern film footage in order to understand their need for thrills considering their positions in life.

Thrillionaires would include:
Space tourists: initial resistance from Nasa to have Russian Soyuz deliver them to ISS on grounds of un-American and interference with crew duties. The main launcher has been through Space Adventures. Cost around $20 million

1. Dennis Tito 2001, American businessmen and former JPL scientist.
2. Mark Shuttleworth, 2002, South African/Brit, Software specialist spent eight days participating in experiments related to AIDS and genome research.
3. Gregory Olsen, 2005 American, former scientist/businessman, conducted several experiments in remote sensing and astronomy. Doesn't like the term space tourist.
4. Anousheh Ansari 2006, Iranian American engineer. Her family contributed the funds for the Ansari X Space prize which SpaceShip One won in 2004. First female Muslim in space. Coined the term 'spaceflight participant'. perform a series of experiments on behalf of the European Space Agency.
5. Charles Simonyi 2007/9 Hungarian American. Software engineer, formerly at Microsoft. Worth $1 Billion. Licensed amateur radio operator
6. Richard Garriott. 2008 American Brit. Video games designer. Second second-generation space traveller and the first offspring of an American astronaut to go into space. Took part in several education outreach efforts
7. Guy Labiberte due Oct 2009, Canadian. Founder and CEO of Cirque du Soleil. Worth $2.5 Billion.

Space racers and adventurers:
1. Sir Richard Branson (adventurer and Virgin Galactic). Worth $2.5 billion
2. Sergey Brin (Google founder and Space Adventures investor –sent 5 into space- his own flight in 2011) $12.0 billion.
3. Paul Allen (owns 3 sports teams and sole investor of Spaceship One -2004) $10.5 billion.
4. Elon Musk (co-founder of PayPal and SpaceX for human space travel) $328 million in 2005.
5. Robert Bigelow (hotel and aerospace entrepreneur), inflatable space habitats.
6. Jeff Bezos (Amazon founder) and in 2004, he founded a human spaceflight startup company called Blue Origin. $10 billion.
7. Lawrence Ellison (Founder of Oracle and Yacht racer, but after winning the 1998 Sydney to Hobart Yacht Race in which a storm killed 6 other sailors never raced again). $22.5 billion.
8. Steve Fossett (aviator, mountain climber, dog sledded, sailor, and adventurer and the first person to fly solo non-stop around the world in a balloon). He set 116 records in five different sports, 60 of which still stood, as of June 2007. Usual faked death reports.

What makes them want to take the risks? Is it for more fame, money, and challenges? Is it to leave a lasting legacy? Is charity work not enough? Are there no other outlets for their energy and wealth? In some cases, are their lives worth the risks?

For those who aren't into high-stakes physical adventure:
1. Bill Gates (founder of Microsoft, humanitarian Bill and Melinda Gates Foundation) $40 billion.
2. Donald Trump (Real Estate mogul, The Apprentice star and Miss Universe Pageant owner) $1.6 billion.
3. Pierre Omidyar (Ebay founder and philanthropist) $3.6 Billion.
4. Roman Abramovich (Oilman, Sports team owner, and recent governor of Russian province) $8.5 billion.
5. Ted Turner (CNN founder, sports team owner –donated $1 Billion to U.N. in 1998) $2.3 billion.

What drives them and would they consider the Thrillionaire lifestyle? Or are they enjoying a different type of Thrillionaire buzz with charities, donations, and owning sports teams and property?

Audience draw:
These are the rich and famous putting their money where their mouth is. This oligarchy of wealthy adventurers may inspire people or simply reinforce the notion that rich kids can play with their rich toys, while the rest of us simply stay on Earth. Others may feel that it proves that money can't buy everything, if Thrillionaires feel they have to live on the brink of danger to feel alive. Is there a psychological element in proving themselves or just an inbuilt sense of adventure? Thrillionaire will search for the answers that the audience and perhaps the Thrillionaires seek themselves.

Filming: Serious interviews, agendas and business, save space industry, lower costs for Earth orbit, moon and Mars missions Quirky eccentrics, humour, bored boys (and one woman) with toys.

End.

12/Oct/2009

The Elemental Human

2020 vision
This had first been sent to **Five** in November 2007 and then to **Mentorn TV** on 07.01.08. Again Five had some good advice and that was this was more suitable as a BBC show as it was more science-orienated, but **Five** tended to steer away from straight science and if anything their output was more engineering focussed. So, I sent it into the **BBC**, but no dice. Though I was told not to regurgitate shows that had been rejected, I refashioned this for **Windfall**.

Premise: An innovative look at the human condition through the medium of the elements.

The Elemental Human will delve into the essential ingredients of human beings and try to answer: Are we really just the sum of our elemental parts. There are over one hundred elements, some natural, some man-made, some found only in the cosmos and others absorbed from the earth. **The Elemental Human** will investigate our elemental heritage and how we are using elements to create the technology to sustain us?

Channel:
The Elemental Human will be a 3 x 60 minute BBC 2 series, part of their Consumer Science strand combining human evolution and BBC 2's popular earth science strand in the 9pm slot. **The Elemental Human** will be well-placed for BBC2 as it is a big idea incorporating evolution, technology, and the natural world that we are literally a part of.

USP:
* Use of the Periodic Table to highlight the scale and diversity of human composition.
* Use and adaptation of two proven Windfall 'brands' of imagery: Blue framework CGI from Big, Bigger, Biggest to build a virtual human subject. Use of 3D CAT scan to navigate and pin-point areas of interest in human subject.
* Televised use of SEM (Scanning Electron Microscope) on human parts to illustrate element concentrations and functions.

Talent:
A narrator will provide the constant thread between presenters knowledgeable in chemistry, physics, biology, social history, and futurology.

Format:
The first programme will take a light-hearted look at the elemental structure of the human body from head to toe (using above technology). As each bodily structure (bones, tissue, and blood, etc) is examined the elemental composition, relevance, and function is explained.

The second programme will reveal man's literal appetite for technology (e.g. zinc pills, metallic/ceramic/silicon implants, pace makers). We will discuss the medical and social effects using technology has had on us (e.g. health, conflict, financial), even from early historic medical practices. Where possible, this will be accomplished through global statistic records, anecdotal evidence, and film footage.

The third programme will examine the question: Are these elements the end-all of humans? Do their interactions explain our behaviour and consciousness? How has the elemental composition of humans changed from the past? And in the future, can humans change their elemental structure to produce a new human? Will we become more metallic than flesh? Computer imagery and interviews with futurologists will be presented here to illustrate the elemental future of humanity.

Content:
Episode 1 title (?): The Human Star. What does it take to make a human? From the explosive supernovas, which have endowed us with heavy elements, how has the universe shaped us? We all know about carbon, calcium, and iron, etc, that make up the human body, but what about other rare and trace elements within us like selenium, silver, the lanthanides and even gold, etc. What biological role do these elements have?

Episode 2 title (?): The Human Element. We will investigate the human cost of technology, the ever-more exotic materials we use and imbibe during our lives. We will scour the world for materials to make the objects we work and play with (e.g. Tantalum or Coltan in mobiles that fuels the Congo war, copper jewellery which may heal us, uranium miners who dig with their hands to give us electricity and bombs), but what are the long-reaching effects to ourselves and the environment (e.g. cancers, resource wars and enhanced versus sub cultures)?

Episode 3 title (?): The Human Machine. As for the future, we cast a look in the technological crystal ball at the possible condition of the Tomorrow Man and his possible union with technology (e.g. from Wolverine to Borg to Singularity). How has the human elemental condition changed and how will it be in the future? How far are we willing to go to survive and evolve?

Audience:
The Elemental Human will appeal to core BBC 2 audiences hooked on science and discerning viewers looking for educational, fun, and challenging television.

End.

12/Oct/2009

Election

2020 vision
The feedback I got on this is that it was an interesting seed of an idea, but would work better on the web than on TV as it relies on viewer interaction. If it was just a bit of fun and the UN aren't onboard (which they probably wouldn't be), then a website would be perfect vehicle for this. It could be a game where other people can vote on their 'dream cabinet'. So, do you want to play a game? My choices below...

Premise: Out of the whole world, which 12 people would you vote for to form a world government?

After the euphoria of Obama's election how can this experience be recreated around the world, where people would have the choice to vote for their own 'government'? **Election** will investigate the geopolitical, cross-cultural pulse of the world and feeling towards politics. The UN already chooses Goodwill Ambassadors, but why not allow them to be voted by public who can chose their own candidates and vote them in rather than being chosen for them or even unelected. People can vote for anyone alive in politics, celebrities, sportsmen, even ordinary people, etc.

Channel:
Election would be best suited for Channel 4's 9pm slot as a Big Event idea. The final show will be a live event to broadcast the election winners. With the vote being live and results coming in from all over the world, it will be a cross between 'Election Night' and 'Eurovision'. Possible interviews with candidates and winners' acceptance speeches could be included.

USP:

- A global election travelogue with live global election night coverage and results.
- Email, Facebook, Twitter, paper ads, etc publicity campaign and voting.
- Visit to UN to seal endorsement of winners as world ambassadors

Talent:
One studio-based host, roving reporters, possibly local or embedded reporters in the region to report back.

Multi-Part Series:
Travelogue around the world, series number tbc. Each programme will be an hour long.

The point:
Besides the Obama phenom, there are also The Elders: The formation of this new independent political force went almost unnoticed in 2007, yet they could be the prelude to a new world political movement. Elected from elder statesmen from around the world, headed by Nelson Mandela, The Elders are an impartial group that could mediate and troubleshoot in certain global situations. If successful, could they replace the unwieldy UN and become the legitimate and dominant global political force themselves? Current members include: Desmond Tutu, Jimmy Carter, Muhammad Yunus, Graca Machel, Ela Bhatt, Lakhdar Brahimi, Li Zhaoxing, Kofi Annan, Mary Robinson, Gro Brundtland, Fernando H. Cardoso, with an empty chair for Aung San Suu Kyi. Yet, the group does not seem to have been formed or have any influence on world affairs. If people could have control over their government, who would they freely vote for?

Election would seek trends in future for voting (e.g. online technology, non-standing governments, candidates chosen by people, etc). The results could be compared to national political elections and popular reality TV show percentage votes. **Election** could serve as a Social experiment to see and appreciate the global population's similarities or differences.

Audience:
Election would produce unprecedented audience participation beyond TV, culminating in a live TV event. This fun yet educational and thought provoking view on voting may encourage more voting and change election systems around the world. Let the voting begin...

End.

My election choices:

President William Shatner
Vice President: Angelina Jolie
Defence: Mr. T
NASA: Robert Zubrin
Foreign Affairs: Naomi Klein
Press office: Geri Halliwell
Business Czar: Sir Richard Branson
Science: Prof. Stephen Hawking
Atheist Pope: Richard Dawkins
Architecture: Zaha Hadid
Futurology: Ray Kurzweil
Climate: Bjorn Lomborg

14/Oct/2009

The Real Mentalist Files

Premise:
Following the popularity of Five's The Mentalist, this revealing and personal programme will follow real life Mentalists as they work and perform as entertainers and investigators.

Channel:
The Real Mentalist Files will be a Five programme to coincide with the next series of The Mentalist and would complement Five's existing programmes The FBI Files and The Real CSI.

USP:

Talent:
Colourful, real-life Mentalists will reveal the tricks of the trade and reveal why their skills are uniquely to aid in police or investigative work.

Format:

Content:
Issues to be looked at: Communication/Visual evidence (Physiognomy), cold reading (FACS –Facial Action Coding System), Performance, investigations, Profiler and criminal psychologists, 'psychics', actual police cases, and interviews.

Audience:
Five's audience, dedicated to The Mentalist and those favouring real procedural cases will be drawn to this programme.

End.

18/Oct/2009

Antarctican Archaeology

2020 vision

My pitch to **Windfall** was: Whilst reading the last Broadcast mag, I came across **History**'s call for programmes. I had thought about doing this as a one-off doc seeing the British Empire from an Antarctic point of view with this being a series spin-off. I had applied for the Polar Studies MPhil course at Cambridge (but didn't get the grade) But I made a few contacts there and in Australia. I'm sure a new archaeology series not tied to Europe, but involving Brit history (whalers, sealers & explorers), would be of interest.

The feedback was based on experiences in the US - one comment we got was 'ice doesn't rate'!! 'Apparently people don't like to look at a white screen! Crazy huh? So, in short, good idea. Look for a presenter/archaeology team that could make the programme gripping even on the days they don't find anything. Time Team works because Tony and the crew are so fab. In the treatment I wanted to know more about what they might find and what challenges they might face working in those conditions.'

Premise**:** The untold human stories of Antarctica through archaeology. From the first attempts to discover the Southern Continent to modern day scientists living in the shadow of the frozen continent, an existing team of archaeologists will continue their work in archaeology and heritage work in preserving the Antarctican past. And while there is an over-arching big history to be told of early Whalers, sealers, and explorers, they have also left behind many artefacts that will tell many personal stories.

Channel:

Antarctic Archaeology will be a History (Channel) programme, following the exploits of archaeologists and heritage workers in the cold fields of the Antarctican environs. This series would complement History's 'Ice Road Truckers' who operate within the north Polar Regions. The logistical challenges of filming and working in the Southern Ocean and Antarctic Regions will be a tremendous, yet rewarding experience to tell the stories of those who laboured hard to make a living, much like the modern 'Ice Road Truckers'.

USP:
1. Previous contacts with Antarctic workers from Australia and the Scott Polar Research Institute, Cambridge.
2. Introduce a new element in history and archaeology from new perspective and location.

Talent:
The series will be led by a seasoned Polar worker.

Format:
Antarctican Archaeology will feature less archival footage and more artifactual elements to tell the story of early whalers, sealers, and explorers and their attempts to feed, fuel, finance, and bring glory to their countries. This series will focus on a team of colourful and hardy Polar archaeologists from around the world as they plan season work, converge together and travel to Antarctica, work on the Antarctic Islands, Peninsula and seas. There is also scope to trace and interview existing relatives of those whalers and explorers and breath life into black and white photos, letters, and personal items.

Content:
The general timeframe will be from 1699 (Edmund Halley's voyage) to modern day. The 'Antarctic Time Team' series will follow the team as they make new discoveries about past explorations and whaling, survive the harsh conditions, and record the effects of climate change on their environment and careers. Each series would comprise a season's work covering pre- and post-work travel and any results.

Audience:
An Antarctican-based series will introduce the audience to a new historical perspective and the unfamiliar territory of Antarctica.

End.

19/Oct/2009

The Seven Trials of Early Man

2020 vision
Incomplete idea, I found while researching old emails. Much of this would lend itself to a new series I would call '21st Century Caveman' and put modern day people in cavemen situations, living, dressing, hunting, manufacturing tools, etc, like the good old days. There are TV shows doing this now, so I will a little ahead of the time.

Content:

Disaster management:
The Laetoli Footprints from 3.6 million years ago in Tanzania are a testament to early Man's survival instincts. The footprints were preserved in a sandwich of volcanic ash and represent the escape from or awe at the explosive event as they stood and watched the fireworks. Did they successfully escape? Where did they go? The footprints are enigmatic reminders that natural disasters were a constant threat to early man.

Water sports:
We are an aquatic ape due to our early ancestors taking to the water either to swim or build crude rafts. How did Early Man get to Australia? At its shortest, the open water between prehistoric Australia/New Guinea (Sahul) was at least 100 km from South East Asia/Indonesia (Sundra). Surviving the dangerous open seas without proper sea-worthy craft, either by paddling or drifting in high waves would have been awe-inspiring, even more so if swimming were involved. Early man survived his trial by water.

Exploration:
As early man headed off to new horizons, what fate awaited him? He would have had to live off the unfamiliar land and not poison himself or get eaten by unknown predators. Leaving the comfort of home would have necessitated navigation skills, leadership, and intelligence. As early man spread out and colonised the world, each journey, each settlement was a trial of survival skills and human ingenuity.

End.

23/Oct/2009

On Trial: Henry VIII

2020 vision
I was told such topics would wander into David Starkey territory so the idea wasn't used. Wonder what ever became of Starkey?

Premise: Henry VIII is conjured up to face charges for Anglican crimes against Catholicism.

In this surreal docu-drama, the Archbishop of Canterbury, Dr. Rowan Williams defends the former King against the charges brought against him by the current Pope Benedict XVI, before the 'reunification' of Catholicism and Anglicanism. This re-imagining of history combining current news and historical events will place the trial into a modern context. **On Trial** serves to place Anglicanism on trial for its split from the Catholic Church under Henry VIII and also to denote that Anglicans will be on trial when they reconvert.

Channel: History (or if too surreal) Channel 4.

USP: Part of the Henry VIII 500th year coronation anniversary celebration.

Talent: Actors and news footage

Format: On Trial will be a one-off, 90' special where a Judge and Jury will sit in deliberation of the evidence against Henry VIII. Both the Defence (the Archbishop) and the Prosecutor (The Pope) will make their cases and Henry will also take the stand.

Content:
The Court case takes place at the Old bailey. The Charges are:
1. Henry VIII charged on 2 counts of uxoricide and 2 counts of unlawful divorce.
2. Precipitating Anglican split from Catholicism and future Northern Ireland wars.
3. Unlawful breach of human rights and discrimination against Catholic Monarchs, Members of Parliament, and people.

4. Unlawful possession of Catholic churches and lands; Right of re-possession.
5. Split from Catholicism encouraged Darwinism, homosexuality, female clergy, etc.

The Archbishop's Defence case: Innocent plea.
1. King Henry VIII acted in best interest of country and acted of his own time. Murder charges to be dropped; divorces were annulments.
2. The effects of 'reunification'/re-conversion will undermine the succession of Monarchy.
3. The effects of 'reunification'/re-conversion will split the Church even further.
4. The effects of 'reunification'/re-conversion will affect relationship with Jews and Muslims, the latter which will feel surrounded by the new Holy Atlantic Empire.
5. The effects of 'reunification'/re-conversion will destabilise global and EU politics.

In the midst of the court case will be media claims of a deal for the Archbishop to turn on Henry VIII in bid to become the second British Pope ever. With Prince Charles and Tony Blair agitating for the same post, what will the Archbishop do? Also, the real special relationship between US Presidents and God becomes apparent. Will the President take orders from the Pope? Only if the Pope is American.

How will the jury vote? What will be the future of the world in the event of the re-unification of Anglicanism and Catholicism? The outcome of the Trial of Henry VIII will have far reaching consequences for the future of Britain.

Audience:
On Trial: Henry VIII will be a fun, but provocative debate on the state of religion in Britain as Anglicanism struggles to gain members, include homosexual and female clergy, and reach an ambivalent alliance with the Pope. As a docu-drama delivered with humour and interspersed news clips, the audience will be able to understand the underlying complex issues without feeling excluded by the subject matter, patronised by partisan TV debates, or preached to by talking heads.

End.

24/Oct/2009

Lost: Never Found

Premise: An ambitious scientific mission to Antarctica to find the body of explorer Captain Lawrence Oates.

Can the whereabouts of Oates be discovered after all these decades using modern technology? This programme will combine docu-drama of the events leading up to his disappearance with modern explorers/scientists' efforts to find him. Journeying to find his lost remains will also serve to highlight his sacrifice and service to his country.

Channel: History

USP:

Talent: Narrator, actors, scientific team

Format: Lost: Never Found will be a one-off 90' special. It will be a 3-part story, detailing the 1912 mission, the modern team efforts, and the scientific analysis and results.

Content:
Captain Lawrence Oates, who famously sacrificed himself during the 1912 Polar expedition of Scott. Oates' body has been lost to the Antarctic Ice; a cairn placed near to the alleged place of death, but no body had been found.

While the general area of Oates' death may be known, his remains are not. The deep snow and ice have covered him, and ice may be drifting in different directions at differing speeds over the century. Tracing such changes will be difficult over such lengthy periods. Can computer programmes be made to compensate for changes? How deep can remote sensing and ground penetrating radar go? Will they be able to pinpoint anomalies through the ice? What would be the consequences and moral issues in exhuming any artefacts or the remains of the Antarctican hero? Will he be reburied where he lay or repatriated with Scott in their icy tomb?

Audience:
History buffs, adventurers, and followers of history mysteries will be interested in the Boys' Own adventurers and derring-do.

End.

28/Oct/2009

Thrillionaire: The Extreme Thrill Seekers
(2nd concept)

2020 vision
Unfortunately, in the end we couldn't use the Thrillionaire name as it is copyrighted by Nik Halik and we weren't allowed its use. He had a website devoted to himself as the Thrillionaire and a book about his adventure in space his book (though ulitmately he did not fly into space). It would have been great if we followed him on his quest to the ISS and get insights into what makes him a Thrillionaire, but ultimately the legalities deterred us.

Our other target, Steve Truglia, already had media for his space jump. I had also contacted www.spaceadventures.com for information on orbital spaceflight clients (Space Tourists) and even the makers of the Moller M400 Skycar for a series. This was the last show I developed while I was on placement.

Premise: The mega-sized dreams, projects, and adventures of millionaires seeking extreme thrills.

Being a multui-millionaire is not enough. Hostile takeovers are not de rigueur anymore. One has to show the world that they are ready to use their riches to explore all avenues of thrills, exploration, and extreme investment. This has culminated in the rise of the self-mega-funded adventurer, the super-elitist collector, and space tourist. But why are these super well-off putting their own lives unnecessarily under threat –for the greater good of mankind or in pursuit of vain-glorious passions? This programme will attempt to gain an insight into the mind of the Thrillionaire.

Channel:

Format:
This 6-part 60' programme will explore the phenomenon of the Thrillionaire. Through first-person presentation and presented narratives, the audience see the incredible mega-rich projects and hobbies that multi-millionaires undertake because they have the cash to splash and egos to match.

Content:

Episode 1: Space Explorer

From initial resistance from NASA to have Russian Soyuz deliver the Space Tourists to the ISS on the grounds of being un-American and interference with crew duties, the Thrillionaires have succeeded in making it into space. The main launcher has been through Space Adventures. Costs for a Space Tourist ride are estimated to be a whopping $20 million per person. Seven have made it thus far, and Sergey Brin, Google co-creator and Space Adventures investor, is due to join the magnificent seven in 2011.

(Anousheh Ansari, the only female space explorer, so far, could offer her insights as Brin is followed on his training.)

Episode 2: Abramovich's Navy

Roman Abramovich's fleet of yachts are about to be joined by, not one, but two submarines. The 118-ft Seattle 1000 has been ordered from the leading manufacturer US Submarines at a cost of £13m with running yearly costs of £1m. The second sub from the same company will be the smaller £3m 65-ft Nomad 1000, which will be able to dock with one of Abramovich's other mega yachts. Having never been a naval officer, what is the reason for Abramovich needing a veritable armada that would make third-world countries look on with envy?

(Would there be access to seeing the boats under construction?)

Episode 3: Space Jump

Steve Truglia is a stunt man extraordinaire. The former soldier and extreme sportsman has starred in numerous films, been set on fire the longest, freedived the deepest, and looped the loop in a car on a giant scale. As the Action Unit Director in the UK, Truglia has set the example with the records to prove it. Now he is ready for the ultimate challenge, yet. From the edge of space, protected only by a spacesuit, Truglia will attempt to break the world record high altitude parachute jump set in 1960 by Joe Kittinger. Will he succeed? What preparation will he need? Steve Truglia may not have the billions, but he has all the right stuff of the definitive Thrillionaire.

(Steve's website and he gives lectures about his stunts:

http://spacejump.co.uk/

Episode 4: Yacht Wars
Larry Ellison once quit yacht racing after six men died on another boat while he raced and won the 1998 Sydney Hobart race. He has since resurfaced with a vengeance with a revolutionary new $10m 90-ft trimaran to challenge fellow bio-tech Billionaire Ernest Bertarelli on the high seas and in the courts. At stake is for the right for Ellison to be the rightful challenger in the 33rd America's cup in February 2010, which has eluded his grasp. With some legal wrangling lingering, it looks set that the Billionaires will finally race head to head. This is a personal duel. This means more than national or professional bragging rights. This is a Billionaire's pride at stake...
(Build up and coverage of the race could be included).

Episode 5: Mile High Wedding Planner
On June 20, 2009, Space Tourist and Brit Billionaire gaming guru Richard Garriott carried out another first by officiating at the first ever wedding to be held in zero gravity. Garriott, the co-founder of Zero Gravity Corp (ZERO-G), a company offering weightless flight experiences in a specially modified Boeing 727-200 aircraft, G-Force One, performed the ceremony after being ordained by a California church. As Garriott has retreated away from computer games, has Zero G and space become his new toy?
(YouTube clips of wedding exist. Interview with Garriott?)

Episode 6: Thrillionaire Junkie
Nik Halik has it all; the money, fame and adventurous lifestyle. His biography is called: The Thrillionaire. He's climbed the highest peaks, chased tornadoes, walked on the Titanic (With Garriott), skydived and paid $30m to be the back up to Garriott as a space participant. So what will he do next for his next Thrillionaire kick?
(Halik has started a website for other Thrillionaires and could be the 'go-to' guy on the inside track on who is next on the wild side).

Thrillionaire will ask: what makes them want to take the risks – more fame, money, challenges, or a lasting legacy? Are there no other outlets for their energy and wealth?These are the rich and famous putting their money where their mouth is. This oligarchy of wealthy adventurers may inspire people or simply reinforce the notion that rich kids can play with their rich toys, while the rest of us simply play in the sand pits on Earth. Others may feel that it proves that money can't buy everything, if Thrillionaires feel they have to live on the brink of danger to feel alive. Is there a psychological element in proving themselves or just an inbuilt sense of adventure? **Thrillionaire** will search for the answers that the audience and perhaps the Thrillionaires seek themselves.

Audience:
Thrillionaire will appeal to those who love real, big unattainable adventures. The first-person narrative approach, in some cases, will offer the viewer more personal insights than straight interviews, allowing the audience to share in being on the edge of an out-of-this-world experiential moment.

End.

01/Nov/2009

Six Degrees

2020 vision

While I had left Windfall Films without a job, I still sent in a few ideas. This was originally created 19/10/09 and then updated following feedback: 'You need to mention right up top that your version of the game aims to highlight how, although the world has got smaller, there are still some massive extremes out there – between climates, cultures, rich and poor etc. This series takes a game and gives it social purpose: the point of it is to highlight these disparities in an entertaining way. As far as I could tell there was no overt mention of these 'clashes' in the summary page -only in the individual episode outlines.'

Premise: Follow six diverse people on a global mission to find a far-flung stranger within six steps or less.

Is everybody connected to someone else in the world by an average of six steps? Six degrees of separation became popular in the 1990s as part of the 'small world phenomenon' being studied by scientists. In 1994, a game was devised in which Hollywood actor Kevin Bacon could be linked to any other Hollywood actor within six links or less (example right) through the movies he had made with mutual actors.

In 2003, filmmaker Lucy Leveugle set out to discover how many degrees of separation stood between her and a nomadic Mongolian herdsman, Purev-Ochir Gungaa. She made it in nine steps. Now, the urban myth continues to be tested in this bold new series. A mix of people from diverse geographical and cultural backgrounds learn for themselves whether the world has really got smaller or if the extremes in wealth, culture, education, politics, and even climate still continue to act as barriers to even the strictest test of Six Degrees. Our test-subjects will contact someone who knows someone, who knows someone else, who will know another someone, who will attempt to help them cross the world and through the invisible fences that separate an otherwise connected world. Their journey from one niche extreme to another will lead into unknown realms of self-discovery.

Channel: Channel 4

USP:
Six Degrees would introduce a twist in the familiar myth and social experiment.

Format:
Six Degrees will be 6 x 60' programmes. Each programme will feature a specific individual on their journey, charting their routes and number of degrees taken to reach their ultimate destination. Their initial departure point and destination person will be known and it will be up to the largesse of strangers to direct them on to the next probable shared connection in the chain. A narrator will provide links between celebrities.

Content:
Using helpful computer graphics, the narrator will explain the rules. As each person is introduced, they are handed an envelope. The envelope will have an A4 portrait photo of the destined target, their name, and village/town in whichever country. No other details will be provided.

The tricky part is the first contact: where to start? Who to ask? Where to go? The personality will only be able to use information from the first person suggested by each new contact. They cannot use computer searches, mobiles, or direct contact. None of the intervening six degrees can be family or extended family members (e.g. in-laws, cousins, step family, etc). The ensuing journey will be totally organic, their route necessarily random and their mode of travel just as haphazardly planned.

In a normal Six Degrees narrative, the personality would travel alone to meet those contacts. But in this version, there is scope for Personality X to spontaneously encourage some or all of her contacts to travel together meeting the last one in Tierra del Fuego. Multiple travellers will introduce a frisson of colourful histories, cultures, and characters into a shared Six Degree experience. It will be voyeuristic TV as people are seen to up sticks in an instant to travel with or to a Celebrity and discover how isolated or connected they really are.

Programme examples (in no particular order):

Programme 1:
From the Polar desert, an Inuit from the frozen Canadian North has to meet a camel herder in the Ethiopian Afar, the hottest place on Earth. His world is literally melting, so he will set out to raise awareness of his plight. He carries with him a specially-designed flask full of snow to present to the herder. Will the snow stay intact? What will the herder make of it? Is it a mission too far? Will they find common bonds? We follow the Inuit from -30°C to over 100 ° C within Six Degrees.

Programme 2:
An Aborigine who paints the moon is given the mission of meeting Neil Armstrong, the first man on the moon. Notoriously reclusive and camera shy, will Neil Armstrong consent to a private meeting and to be presented with a work of Dreamtime art representing the moon? Will the Aborigine believe Armstrong has stood on the moon or even know who he is? Legends of the Aborigine moon meets Western science as a member of one of the oldest indigenous tribes goes in search of the man who has travelled the furthest from Earth, within six giant leaps.

Programme 3:
A popular, but little-known-internationally Celebrity from UK has to meet A-list Celebrity in Hollywood of whom she is a big fan. This can only be accomplished through non-celebrity/unfamiliar contacts who are also fans of the A-lister (e.g. no agents, fixers, or other industry wags). Can she make it, present her business card, and get a valued autograph, interview, or just five precious minutes in the presence of a Hollywood great? Hollywood is the stuff of legend, but will the Six Degrees myth live up to its legendary status.

Programme 4:
With the World Cup approaching in South Africa, an aspiring young football player from the townships will attempt to go on the journey of a lifetime and meet a football legend. Will he meet an African legend or an International superstar? How will he do it? Who can help him? Will he get to play a game with the professional? With his parent/guardian in tow, the boy begins his trip away from the world he knows and into the big league.

Programme 5:
Double Jeopardy: A young UK gang member from a tough estate and a Women's Institute member of have to meet a prisoner in the US on Death Row. They can either travel together or use each others' contacts.

What will their reaction be? Will People choose to help them speak to a convicted murderer? What will they learn on their journey as they realise they are six steps away from being on the other side of the bars?

Programme 6:
A battery chicken farm worker in rural China travels to meet one of the last remaining Faberge family members, Sarah, in Russia. Who could she possibly know to connect her to the Faberges? What would they have in common? From her poor farm in China, how will she react to the riches and treasures on display? The Chinese farmer will present a natural egg of her own, hopefully which will be decorated Faberge style as a reward for her journey.

Programme 7:
An Amazonian Shaman swaps the remote, lush jungle for the concrete jungle of Tokyo and its 28 million people, where he must meet a sorcerer of technology. What will he make of robots and high-tech gadgets? How will he cope with the noise, pollution, crowds and alien technological culture? What will he take back with him? From low tech to high tech in Six Degrees.

Programme 8:
Politician Michael Portillo or Boris Johnson's dad, Stanley, must find his way to North Korea to meet Kim Jong-il. Will he be able to find the six non-political connections between himself and the Supreme Leader? Will he be able to make it across the border? What threats might he face? What will he say to the Leader, if he is allowed to meet him? The contrast between Western lifestyles and North Korean lives will be tested Six Degrees style.

Audience:
How close are we to knowing a celebrity or far-flung stranger - one step, two steps, dozens? If a herder in Outer Mongolia is six degrees or less from a Western celebrity then how closely related is our global village? Six Degrees will attract family audiences interested in celebrity travelogues with a difference and those interested in the six degrees mythology. For a journey of a lifetime, just go Six Degrees.

End.

04/Nov/2009

The Event: My Backyard Nuclear Reactor

2020 vision

This came out from my article on The Waste of Nuclear Waste and my letter to James Lovelock and the Environmentalists for Nuclear Energy (EFN). The EFN are a not-for-profit organization created in 1996. Initially based in France, but spreading worldwide, they have over 16,000 members and supporters in 65 countries. After my letter, I had an invitation to the EFN annual meeting that November from Bruno Comby, President of the EFN. At the time, I thought it would be a good idea to go along and interview them, but upon reflection, I changed it around as it would be a bunch of talking heads. However, both James Lovelock and the EFN preseident, Bruno Comby, have gone on record to say they would accept highly radioactive material on their land to heat their home and water (as chronicled in my first volume *Musings of an Infovore*).

So I thought why not try that out? We have nuclear waste going to waste, why not put it to good use? However, in my correspondence with Bruno Comby a main problem is the high cost of the handling and transport of nuclear materials. Such an experiment could challenge the big bad image of all nuclear waste being a hazard and lead to new uses of nuclear energy.

As nuclear energy is an emotive subject, I wondered if this would make a good doc, with these environmentalists putting their view forth, which runs contrary to other envionmentalists' claims about safe, clean nuclear energy. Also, with James Lovelock's new book out at the time, we could have a doc, documenting his 'conversion' to the nuclear cause. I was not sure about access to him, but it couldn't hurt to ask and the EFN were not averse to having a doc about them.

The feedback for this was - 'Presumably we couldn't actually risk nuclear material leaking out – so given we'd have to use a mocked up house or controlled environment, can you think of any tests we could do or demos to show what's happening that don't just involve Geiger counters!' - I could have, but in the end the legalities of procuring, transporting and installing a small chunk of radioactive material in a back garden to power a house would have been unfeasible. Perhaps an idea ahead of its time.

Premise: Famously, James Lovelock has publicly offered to accept a cubic meter worth of waste nuclear material to heat his home. Would anyone else?

My Back Yard Nuclear Reactor will put this proposal to the test. This experiment will gauge nuclear bias, study recycled resource management, and test a potential new home energy source. Can nuclear waste be the next big thing in the green revolution?

Channel:
My Back Yard Nuclear Reactor will be a television first and ripe for Channel 4.

USP:
Never before attempted experiment on such a level.

Talent:
Possibly Dick Strawbridge for his presenting, engineering skills and green credentials, reporting on the backyard nuclear facility.

Format:
One 60 minute episode: The initial set-up and trial, negotiations with the nuclear facility for material and transport costs, and the health and safety aspects will be detailed here, featuring the trial period (filmed over several weeks), ongoing analysis by environmentalists and nuclear scientists who will assist and judge the success or failure of the experiment. There is scope within the programme; the Event, after 'the reveal', for a discussion between government officials, nuclear experts, private companies, the public, and other interested parties invited to discuss the relative merits of using such small nuclear material in domestic instances.

Content:
The Nuclear House
A house at an undisclosed location will be chosen to house the UK's first residential nuclear material reactor, consisting of a meter square block of vitrified nuclear waste, wrapped in a concrete seal. A crane will be shown lifting the block into position in the back garden where it will sit above ground, protected from cosmic rays and the outside environment.

Strawbridge and his team will assist in installing the waste reactor and investigating how safe and functional the set-up is, testing the ground around the material for leaks, and the house for any contamination. The nuclear family of husband wife and couple children will be filmed living their daily lives, using the newly installed energy source. Even the kids will be shown 'decorating' the concrete block with paint and a façade to make it less austere and imposing (above).

Every day, the family will check the block with Geiger counters and check for cracks or other signs of damage. Scientists will check every so often too. The family in the Nuclear House will have a video diary of the benefits or disadvantages that the reactor is bringing. After a month, the test will be over and all the tests will be analysed. Strawbridge will then announce that the next programme will reveal the secrets as to how this was made possible.

All safety and responsible precautions will be taken when filming and handling nuclear material.

At the end of the programme, 'the reveal' will acknowledge that it is prohibited to have nuclear waste outside of a power station and that the Nuclear House was staged. In fact, the house was receiving power not from nuclear waste, which is a bona fide technological concept, but from the waste heat of a nuclear reactor, which has vast more amounts of energy to give through waste heat than nuclear waste. This cogeneration scheme can be used to power more homes at a cheap price. The waste material the programme was advocating was not nuclear, but waste heat.

A discussion with politicians, nuclear experts, other experts, and companies would take place within the programme to discuss the events of the programmes and the ramifications of residential nuclear power and cogeneration.

<u>Audience:</u>
This fun, daring, and demonstrative experiment will challenge our fears about nuclear energy on a personal level. The thought of a 'personal' nuclear reactor will be provocative and invite much debate as to its worth and usability. The inner scientist and curious will be drawn to the programme, especially men who may even expect an explosion (there won't be). Sceptics of large scale nuclear power may protest, but a successful trial may sway voters on the safety and need for nuclear power.

End.

My correspondence with Bruno Comby, President of the EFN.

Wed 21/10/2009

Hello Bruno,

Hopefully you'll remember me regarding my article on Helium.com about using nuclear waste to heat water and home and we had a couple of email discussions back in July, regarding this.

Well, I am still writing, but I also now have a two-week placement at a TV production company. Your newsletter regarding EFN's Annual meeting got me thinking about what you had said and I mentioned this to my Development Manager. She is very interested in the fact that you, James Lovelock, and possibly others would volunteer to do this. I have devised a TV programme around this (below) and wondered what you thought of it. If someone volunteered from EFN, could it be done? If not, we would build a mock-up house and try it there. Besides costs, what else would we need to think about. This wouldn't just be a publicity stunt, but a way of showing that nuclear waste could have further uses and not be the gloom and doom of the environment.

I hope this is agreeable to you and I thank you for your time. I look forward to hearing your views.

Regards,
Ray Burke

**

Response from Bruno Comby

From: Bruno Comby
Sent: 23 October 2009
To: ray burke
Subject: Re: TV programme about nuclear waste use

Dear Ray

Thanks for your kind message.

Fundamentally, in theory, it might be possible technically to heat a home with radioactive waste: for example (there are various possible configurations) dig a pit about 10 meters deep 1 meter wide (much like an ordinary well for water a century ago). Put a copper tupe spiraling around where the waste canister will be deposited in the bottom of the pit. Then put the canister inside with all necessary precautions (shielding on the day it is brought and lowered in the pit). Fill with concrete above (a few meters of earth or concrete is enough to stop even the most penetrating gamma rays). If you want to be very safe, put extra shielding around the entire system and add an extra intermediate water circuit so that the water circulating in the copper tupe around the waste is a distinct circuit from the water heating the house).

The heat level will slowly decrease over time (in years) as radioactive elements progressively decay. The system will be hotter the first years than afterwards, but any extra-heat in the early years or on hot days can be easily dispersed to the atmosphere. In winter the hot water will be sent to the central heating system of the house, providing free heating, and the excess heat would be sent to the atmosphere (the extra heat might also be used to heat a block of earth or a pool of water to store the heat until winter - see "seasonal heat storage" on google). Everything can be dimensioned so that even if the water stops flowing in the copper tube for some reason, the temperature reached does not rise to the point where the canister melts (with a safety margin) therefore everything remains perfectly contained.

Another design: simply dispose the waste canister above ground with adequate shielding around it (concrete or lead) and recuperate the heat simply by circulating air around the double-tight canister.

Doing this with real waste would not be possible in my opinion in Western european countries because of the numerous regulations and public hysteria about handling radioactive waste. This would probably be possible only in small african or non-democratic country where there are no rules or simple rules about radiation or where rules don't apply (which isn't a good example to follow).

Doing this in a western country with real waste would lead you directly to prison! (and no nuclear operator would ever acccept to deliver the waste to you in the first place).

Therefore to explain the concept in a film if you wish to do so, a fake installation and a simulation should be set up to explain the idea in the media. The waste canister might be very similar in appearance to the real ones but the hot radioactive waste could be replaced by an electrical resistance providing the same amount of heat placed in an empty canister (simulating the heat provided by the waste).

This could be done and be presented as a scientific study of the feasibility of the system and its technical possibilities: how effective is the heat transfer to the copper tubes? what happens (safety and dangerous or non-dangerous temperature reached) if the water cooling stops? There are several possible designs: above ground or underground, using water or air for the heat transfer, the waste being surounded by concrete or other solid shielding or simply air cooled, various types and shapes of canisters could be envisaged...

The authors would certainly be considered as crazy (and public dangers) if working with real waste, but presenting it as a scientific study of the feasibility of a new concept using fake waste would be easier (and still quite a taboo-breaker).

A real house (already existant, therefore free) could be used, and just the fake canister and heat recuperation system placed around it would have to be built (and perhaps connected to the existing floor-heating or central heating system of the house). Air or water heat transfer could be tested.

I don't think this would be economically viable today because the safety rules make any handling of radioactive drums hugely expensive.

If such low temperature recuperation was feasible it would be more justified economically and technically to recuperate the heat thrown out to the atmosphere or rivers around an NPP (2/3 of the heat is rejected and only 1/3 converted to electricity). This represents HUGE amounts of low temp heat that could be used for city heating or for agriculture (heating greenhouses to grow vegetables in winter...). In comparison to this huge release of heat in the environment of an NPP (in pure loss today), the residual heat in the waste is peanuts (but still enough to heat a number of homes for 50 years).

In Tricastin, excess heat from the NPP is used to heat a greenhouse with crocodiles.

A nuclear reactor exclusively for central heating of the city of Grenoble named Thermos was designed (and never built, for political reasons, the design was technically sound) in the early 80's in France. A similar system was indeed built in Sweden and heated an entire district around Stockholm for a few years before the system was stopped for political reasons (rise of the anti-nuke ideology in Sweden). Small reactors have been used for heating some cities in the former USSR. The Temelin reactor in Czech Republic today uses part of its low temp heat to heat the local city rather than river water or the atmosphere (initially a much greater proportion of the low-temp heat was envisaged to heat Prague and/or another nearby large city, the technical and even economics were OK but politically it was not decided).

See attached HTML file about cogeneration with nuclear heat or nuclear reactors used exclusively for heating purposes.

Yours sincerely, with kindest regards.

Bruno Comby

Sun 25/10/2009

Hello Bruno,

Thank you for your reply. There were some very interesting facts there and a lot to take in. My manager is sorting through the details to see what can be done, as there may be another science programme building a house near to a NPP and 'plugging in' to its system, but we don't have precise details as to what they are doing. The cogeneration information and attachment just showed how much could be accomplished if politicians really grasped the mettle and showed some foresight in building/adapting the new NPPs to capture the residual heat.

Thank you again for the information. I hope it can lead to an interesting science documentary.

Regards,
Ray

12/Nov/2009

Celebrity Superbowl

2020 vision
A non-Windfall Films series with my letter to legendary sports pundit Mike Carlson at the end. Carlson was a long-time co-host of NFL shows on Channels 4 and 5, along with Superbowl commentary on the BBC.

Premise: Celebrities and sportsmen play in American Football game. With two American NFL games announced for next year, possibly at Wembley and with sell out crowds, American Football is on the rise.

Here is a chance for celebrities to put their money and bodies where their mouths are and take part in the physical game. There are many sofa-quarterbacks and would-be wide receivers who talk a good game or who wonder what they would be like as a player. The game would be for charities of their choice.

Channel: Five

USP: Never been attempted before.

Talent: Trevor Nelson, Nat Coombs, Martin Johnson, Mike Carlson.... There is also scope for celebrity females to be cheerleaders, learning from professional cheerleaders and adding some sideline cheer for the players.

Format:
In this 2x one-hour programmes, actors, celebrities, politicians, sportsmen, and other selected persons are trained in the game of American Football and will take up positions against a semi-pro/US College Team. Either the entire team can be celebrities or celebrities can be inserted into positions.

Content:
Celebrity Superbowl would consist of 2 x 60' programmes. The first would chronicle the backgrounds, training of the celebrities, choosing their team name and creating jerseys for the big game. They will also keep video diaries of their training from their training camp. The second programme, The 'Superbowl' will be a strictly timed 1 hour game of 15 minute quarters (i.e. no clock stoppages), the highlights of which will be shown on TV. The commentators (to be announced) will also receive comments by Facebook, email and twitter, which you could address later on NFL Live.

The pre-game and half-time shows will have the ubiquitous bands and the cheerleaders could be a girl band and/or other female celebrities.

At the end of the game, a celebrity MVP will be picked and the money raised for charity presented. The post-game thoughts of the celebrities will also be captured through interviews and video diaries.

Audience:

As Five currently has the best NFL coverage and most loyal fans, Celebrity Superbowl would be well-placed in Five with yourself participating as a coach, a role many would revel in seeing you in. The audience for the programme will be watched by its core audience and pick up new viewers through the introduction of the celebrities. Celebrity Superbowl has the potential to be a yearly event, possibly in the run-up to the Wembley NFL games and a sure way to boost American Football's popularity in the UK.

End.

My letter to American sports pundit Mike Carlson for his participation in the show.

Dear Mike Carlson,

Re: CELEBRITY SUPERBOWL

Sorry for the unsolicited message. My name is Ray Burke and I create TV programmes. I am also a NFL fan (NY Giants) and I would like to propose a TV show for you along with Sunset and Vine/Five.

As the name suggests, Celebrity Superbowl will take celebrities (actors, singers, reporters, sportsman, etc) anyone who thinks they can play the game and put them through their paces. The game will be played for a charity of the celebrities' choice and raise more awareness of the game. Celebrity Superbowl will serve as a further introduction to American Football through the auspices of familiar faces and talents in an unfamiliar setting.

I envisage a mixed team of celebrities and BNFL teams against another BNFL (team to be selected or a Probowl-like selection made). While played in the UK, perhaps in the run-up to the Wembley regular-season games, the celebrities can be from any country. Celebrity Superbowl will also highlight the growing British National Football League profile and provide more support for them.

I also envisage you as the coach for the celebrity team and possibly Nat Coombs and Trevor Nelson as the players they think they are, and Natalie Pinkham as the touchline reporter. Celebrity Superbowl will be well-suited for Five's remit, especially as it would be for charity, akin to Soccer Aid matches played by celebrities in aid of many causes. As everyone is well-aware, American Football is a contact sport and perhaps celebrities will be concerned about injuries, but as Five has also 'hosted' *The Games,* while ITV shows *Dancing on Ice* and the BBC *Strictly Come Dancing*, all have their inherent injury dangers. The celebrities will be versed in the rules and on protection to avoid causing and receiving injuries.

I look forward to hearing your response. Celebrity Superbowl is a format that could run in many countries and keep American Football on the agenda. Thank you for your time,

Yours truly,

Ray Burke

06/Apr/2010

21st Century Caveman

2020 vision
A non-Windfall Films series, but I had sent in the idea to my friend and TV presenter Peter Ginn. In October 2009, I had come up with **The Seven Trials of Early Man**, which I then incorporated into this series. Was it by luck or trial and error that they discovered these things? Below, I wanted 'modern humans' to recreate and live in the caveman world.

Premise: A modern group of men and women live the life of the caveman.

Following on from popular 'experiential history' programmes rooted in familiar history, **21st Century Caveman** takes us back to the beginning of history. Five men and five women will experience the caveman life in an isolated, wild location for six nerve-wracking weeks. How will these strangers cope together in the most basic of situations? Their journey will show how far away from Mother Nature we have come and to see if their inner caveman can be found.

Channel: BBC 3

Format: **21st Century Caveman** will be 6 x 60' programmes, filmed over six weeks. Fast-paced and action orientated, the modern cavemen will learn and recreate basic caveman skills from experts, before being abandoned in the wild to survive. The filming and action will be organic, with narration to link scenes and provide information. There will be no dramatic input from scripting, save for a shocking surprise in store for the unwary cavemen.

Content:
The action and drama will be focused on the disparate group from the start as we see them individually abandoned in an unknown location near dark with just the clothes on their backs. The strangers in a strange land will have to initially find each other and bond quickly as darkness falls. Each caveman will have been taught a particular skill and will have to teach the others if they want to survive. The location should have everything they need to survive or they'll have to improvise.

By night fall they will have to create suitable shelter from available raw material and get a hearth going for warmth. Who will be the leader(s) and will others follow? Will they split up to do their individual tasks? Can they learn each others' skills? Will they succeed in making tools and weapons for hunting and fishing? Will tensions rise or will love be found? Will the women hold their own, form cliques, or revert to being subservient homemakers? Will the cavemen bond in time?

For, unbeknownst to the cavemen, another 'hostile' tribe had been dropped in a week before, got to know the territory, and will try their best to sabotage the cavemen's already hard-earned efforts. These face-painted hostiles will intermittently steal food, play drums in the night to keep the cavemen awake, intimidate with animal noises and by throwing objects into camp, and attempt to 'kidnap' an unwary cavewoman. Will our shell-shocked cavemen give up, turn on each other, or protect themselves? This time, there is no walking out of the jungle or escaping the house, they are on their own for six weeks.

Audience: While breaking the familiar pattern of near-history programmes, this will still retain a similar format feel for reality TV viewers. **21st Century Caveman** will appeal to younger audiences through use of young, attractive participants and the social experiment subject material. Male audiences will be attracted by the Ray Mears/Bear Grylls survival qualities. **21st Century Caveman** will put the meat on the bones of practical caveman life.

End.

06/Apr/2010

Trailer Talk

2020 vision
A non-Windfall Films series.

Premise: The Coming Attractions panel quiz show.

Often, the best part of going to a film is to watch the trailers. Trailer Talk celebrates these mini-films from past and present, national and international, in this fun, comedic, mixture of QI, Question of Sport, and Never Mind the Buzzcocks geared for the film generation. Trailer talk will be different to present film preview shows, combining the craze of internet film trailer viewing, entertainment gossip, and the irreverence of witty game shows. Trailer Talk offers 'trailertastic' comedy action.

Channel:

USP: Film trailer not seen on TV in this format before.

Talent:

Format:
Trailer Talk will be an on-going half-hour format programme showing whole or parts of past/current/new film trailers, B-movie/classics, foreign trailers, home-made trailers and asking interesting and/or fun questions about them. The quiz show will take the format of panel show with a host, 2 captains and 2 guest for each side competing to show their knowledge of movie trailers and letting the audience view movie trailers, new, old, and from around the world.

Content:
There are any number of rounds that can be featured:
Picture board -Team members are asked to Guess the film's tagline from the trailer or from the tagline, guess the film. (generation, genre, or geographical)
What happened next? The trailer is stopped at a critical moment of action.

Observation –various questions about items in trailer
Invent better taglines, the funnier the better
Montage: A series of shots from different trailers describe another film
New trailers: smash or trash
General trailer trivia quick buzzer round

Points are awarded for the correct or most interesting answers.

Audience:
Film-goers and film buffs will not have seen anything like this on TV and be drawn to see classic trailers aired. Casual viewers will watch the programme to catch new trailers and enjoy the familiar comedy quiz panel format.

End.

01/Jun/2010

Avatareality

2020 vision

This was first pitched for **Windfall Films** in January 9th 2010, but needed work around the time my placement finished. With the film 'Avatar' being such a success, it may be time to take a closer look into the world of the avatars. I wrote a short letter to Dr. Aleks Krotoski who I thought would be a great presenter for this. I didn't receive a response.

Dear Dr. Krotoski,

RE: AVATAREALITY

My name is Ray Burke and as well as being a writer, I also like to create TV programmes. I have come up with a new programme focussing on computer avatars and after seeing you present 'The Virtual Revolution', I believe you would be a great presenter for Avatareality. I had originally devised the programme while on a two-week work experience trial with Windfall Films, but have revised it since with you as the principal presenter. I hope it is to your satisfaction.

I realise you are not a production company, get many offers such as this, and are very busy, but I hope that the programme attracts you attention so that a production company would pick it up. I thank you for your time and hope to hear from you soon.

Regards,

Ray Burke

Premise: Online life from an Avatar's point of view.

He's your friend during the day, at work, and down the pub; but once home, out of sight, he transforms to become someone or something unrecognisable. His double life is dangerous, secret, exciting, and rewarding, unlike the next day when you see him back to normal, unaware of his guilty passion. Welcome to the life of the Avatar, the chosen face of the computer literati, who live life through their alter egos while gaming, communicating, and escaping online.

Who are these otherworldly people? An Avatar is a personalised computer character to use while interacting with people online. Are they making us anti-social escapists or are they the future 'face' of all social networking? Avatareality will boldly explore another reality not too far away and challenge the stereotypes behind gaming Avatars.

USP: Through computer software and the Avatar host sites, the programme will film interviews in both 'live' and Avatar reality.

Channel: BBC 2

Talent: Presenter:
Dr. Aleks Krotoski http://alekskrotoski.com/ (BBC2 'The Virtual Revolution') would provide the journey thread seeking out reasons why avatars are so omnipresent and whether they affect real lives for better or for worse. In real life and as an Avatar, Dr. Krotoski will seek answers while navigating the various sites. Will having an avatar affect her usual habits and personality?

An expert on online Avatars is Nick Yee, PhD in Communication - The Proteus Effect: Behavioural Modification via Transformations of Digital Self-Representation. His work on demographics within MMORPG (Massively Multiplayer Online Role-Playing Game) is sited in various gaming reports and popular media. He would be a great resource for interviewing and avatar guidance.
(http://www.nickyee.com/daedalus/gateway_demographics.html)

Format: 5 x 30' programmes. **Avatareality** will heavily feature Avatars of Dr. Krotoski and her interviewees, so most 'filming' will be conducted through pc/desktop screens and within the Avatar worlds themselves. Also, some people may want their identities protected via their Avatars or want to maintain themselves in character. Some of the Avatars can speak, others can respond with text over which a narrator will read/translate the words.

Sites to be approached and/or included are: The Sims, World of Warcraft, Second Life, Meez, Gaia online, voki.com, Avatars Anonymous, and Entropia, among others.

Content: Avatareality will consist of five programmes:

Episode 1: Rise of the Avatar.
Through interviews and online avatar graphics Dr. Krotoski will look at the history and creation of the avatar. We will answer the questions –why do we need them? Studies show that gamers identify with their avatars as though they were themselves. How are avatars used? Are anonymous avatars better at socialising than face to face meetings? How secure are Avatars in maintaining identity and data protection? Our experts will go through the demographics of avatar users and see the trends and patterns emerging.

Episode 2: Avatar Culture.
There is no denying that online communities have a culture all their own. How do avatars enable this? What are the similarities and differences between avatar cultures, politics, spirituality, and economics? How are cultures built? Who owns and earns the most in currency and territory? Our Avatar guides and experts will navigate their way through the various worlds and find out which cultures are the best.

Episode 3: The Sex Life of the Avatar.
Dr. Krotoski investigates the dirty habits of the Avatar. Avatars offer the online user the chance to extend their illicit habits or to re-invent themselves to their new community. Avatars on some sites have sex or encourage abnormal behaviour. Does this affect them in the real world or is this just online fantasy? How can online sexual behaviour lead to real world criminal charges? How can online systems stop children or capture paedophiles from using Avatars for grooming? Interviews with real or Avatar sex addicts will discuss their reasons for their online proclivities.

Episode 4: Dark Avatar.
Like any mask, Avatars offer the chance to hide one's identity. Avatars can hide addictions, aggressive behaviour, and abusive habits. Dr. Krotoski

and experts will look at the ways Avatars can hide physical and psychological problems and. Can Avatars be blamed for causing denial syndromes, shifting any problems from the real world into the online world? How can the online bullies and cyber crackers be prevented from abusing fellow online Avatars or creating chaos? Interviews with victims will be sought and how the abusers were dealt with or otherwise.

Episode 5: The Future Avatar.
Avatars are here to stay and like all things created by humans will evolve to meet the current needs of the online user. A to-be-determined futurologist will try and predict the future of the Avatar. Will Avatars stay online and become more popular? Will they even replace certain online and TV presenters and celebrities (e.g. the news reading Ananova)? Or will Avatars become physical manifestations of cars, houses, and ships (e.g. like the futuristic spaceship, Andromeda –pictured below)? The creator of Second Life, Philip Rosedale, believes virtual worlds will become the new internet, but what is the future of our online society? Is there a cyber utopia awaiting or a deceptively sinister online world full of unreal people?

Audience: Avatareality will garner large male audiences in their mid twenties, as 85% of gamers are male (according to Yee). There are many reasons for using an Avatar and this programme will also be a guide for audiences, especially parents who are concerned for their children's online interactions with Avatars. **Avatareality** will reveal the Avatars in full reality.

End.

23/Sept/2010

Sense of Art

2020 vision

The last idea I sent in to Windfall Films. I liked this one quite a bit along with my last offerings 'Six Degrees' and 'Avatareality'. So the TV world never panned out, but I still wrote down ideas following this.

Premise: Take 6 artists. Subject them to fun, daring, and extreme experiences. Produce a work of art related to that experience.

What is art? How is it made? Can anyone make art in any situation? How connected are our senses to the making of art? These and more are some of the questions that will be asked and answered in this series of experimental Adventure Art. The artists will undergo several tests of physical, emotional, and mental endurance in order to assess how they and their art changes, or not, as the case may be. Art will be broken down, sense by sense, to give the artist and viewer a unique insight into the artist and the origins, persistence, and possible future of art.

Channel: Channel 4

USP: Experiential Adventure Art with a difference

Talent:

Various types of visual artists such as painters, sculptors, ceramicists, fashion designers, jewellers, wood workers, graphic designers, musicians/composers, and choreographers, among others will be chosen to undertake the challenges in the series.

Format:

In each of the eight 60' programmes, the presenters will introduce each of the artists, their backgrounds and artistic experiences. Pre-programme, each artist will have been interviewed about their professions and lifestyles and undergone rigorous physical and mental checks in order to assess their suitability for the challenges. In some cases they will produce art before, during, and after each experience; or only during; or some before and after each experience depending on their skill and the experience.

This will not be a contest with judges, or a winner and loser, per se, but an experience to measure the human ability to produce art under non-optimal circumstances. Each piece of art will be reviewed and displayed at the end of the programme. A willing gallery or museum could be chosen to exhibit the art for the public to appreciate, and perhaps buy.

Content:

Episode 1: Exposure – Exposed to two differing sets of natural environments, the artists will attempt to use all their senses in creating a piece of natural art. One setting will be a serene location where quiet contemplation can take place, while the other will involve a forced jungle trek to an unknown location, perhaps a 'Lost City', to recreate a scene in a limited amount of time. We will see how nature affects art and how artists' senses are influenced by their surroundings.

Episode 2: Sensory deprivation – Locked in a sensory deprivation tank, the artists will have a floating, intensely nervy, self-aware, and lonely existence in the darkness for several hours. Once recovered in total darkness, they will remain deprived of their senses by being isolated in a pitch-black room, monitored by infrared cameras. With only touch and their memories remaining, the artist will produce a work of art based on what they imaged in the abyss. What is sense to art or art to the senses when they are disconnected from each other?

Episode 3: Torture cell – Stressed art under extreme pressure will be produced, as each artist is locked in a cell and bombarded almost constantly with white noise, pain shocks, light flashes, and endless-loop music within a sleepless 24 hour period. Stripped of a sense of self-worth, the artists' nightmare experiences will be captured in their particular art form, whether a reminder of their experiences or an escapist's view from a traumatic event. The psychological aspects of art will be tested in the cell, as we discover if art can survive the breakdown of body and mind.

Episode 4: Shamanic trance – Hallucinations, whether through ancient drug potions of tribal shaman, meditation or chanting, fasting or dance exertion, will bring out the primeval, ancestral, aspect of art. The artists will be split up all over the world as they come face to face with the varied practitioners of ancient spiritual arts. The ancient art of cave painting will be revived as the artists embark on an uncontrolled journey of the inner soul, conjuring up their innate abilities to portray the supernatural world and origins of art as never before.

Episode 5: Fear – Deep down, everyone is afraid of something. Whether in a haunted house, perched for a bungee jump, trapped in a snake pit, or covered in spiders, each artist will confront their greatest fear and produce a work of art related to their fear, during or after the event. Fear is a great motivator; fear reveals our strengths and weakness; fear will drive the artists to fail or succeed because of or despite of their phobias. An artist will always have to face their fears at some point, but will this prove to be their breaking point?

Episode 6: Taste – Sensations of taste, smell, and texture, not for the faint-hearted, will be examined after the artists experience different culinary experiences. A restaurant catering for connoisseurs of exotic foods will be the setting for the ultimate meal. Given foods of unknown origins, the artists will attempt to convey the food's qualities through their various artistic talents. The origins of the food will then be revealed and the artists will prepare another piece of art to reconcile their previous artwork to the truth of the food. A taste for art will definitely be required for this visual feast.

Episode 7: Hypnosis – Raw, unconscious, and subliminal artistic actions in motion will be the task in the penultimate test. Under controlled hypnosis, the artists will be summoned to produce a work of art never undertaken by them before or a piece of art they would never consider doing publicly, or a new piece of art they would consider as their greatest feat of artistry, ever. How deep in our subconscious is art? How far can art be psychologically manipulated? While shamanic trance revealed the inner soul, hypnosis will open the locked psyche to the limitless worlds of art.

Episode 8: Live public experience – Performance art as a group or as individuals will be the final event, live. In front of an audience, possibly in a famous art gallery or museum, the artists will produce a new work of art inspired by their experiences. Will the artists be able to perform live with the added emotional content of a live audience milling around and between them, all within the set time-limit of the programme? Will they be able to bring all their experiences into one grand coalescent piece of art or will their senses be deadened after their trials? Where will their sense of art be?

Audience:
Sense of Art is not a normal arts programme, but a new genre of Adventure Art series on the cutting edge of experience. In breaking down art sense by sense, non-artistic viewers and casual viewers will be drawn in by the adventure aspects of the programme. For established, traditional artists or those of a younger disposition or a new age nature, the programme will be a reminder that the concept of art is a shifting intrinsic human quality, which requires far more than our normal senses to create. **Sense of Art** will add to the age-old debates as to what art really is.

End.

31/Jan/2011

Around the World in 80 Farms

2020 vision
This was first an idea in April 2009, but I later updated it as a vehicle for my friend Peter Ginn, from the Victorian Farm/Edwardian Farm series. I had also sent him an idea called **Britain's Best Farm**, travelling around the UK searching for the best worked or eco-friendly farm. He liked the '80 Farms' idea, so I worked more on that trying to figure out the format.

Subsequently, Peter had a new TV project coming up which he put my name in for. I interviewed over a skype link in an internet cafe for the role of a presenter on what would become **Tudor Monestary Farm** in Feb 2013. I didn't get the role, which went to another friend and fellow archaeology classmate Tom Pinfold, who was great in the role.

<u>Premise</u>: Local farms worldwide and their survival

What is a farm in today's world? A lot has changed in traditional farming culture and underneath the mass-producing giants are small, local and unique farms, changing the way in which farmland and produce are used.

Animal farms with sheep, cattle, pigs, chickens, and grain, etc are giving way to fish farms, wind farms, solar farms, historical farms, exotic agriculture, GM crops, silk, and other non-traditional farms all around the world and in different environments.

Around the World in 80 Farms will seek the modern purpose of the farm, its changing role in supplying food and produce and how farmland resources are changing, especially through financial crises and combating Global Warming. The future survival of the local farm is here.

<u>Channel</u>: BBC 2

<u>USP</u>: A unique look at farms around the world.

<u>Talent</u>: Peter Ginn (Victorian Farm) as one of the presenters

Format:
2 formats available (over 1 series):
10 x 60' episodes with 8 farms featured per episode at approx 7' air time for each farm visited.
or
12 x 60' episodes with 7 farms featured per episode at approx 8' air time for each farm visited.

Each episode either features farms in the same country or each episode features a similar farming practice from different countries, with the last episode covering odd ones out.

Content:
Peter will travel the world exploring examples of local and/or unique farming practices. For example, in South America, he will look at the revived raised field farming, terracing, and semi-subterranean farming methods. In other areas, Peter will farm in the desert (Atacama in Chile?), see farmland turned into energy farms of the future, and practice rare farming techniques and lost traditions.

Episodes will showcase the uniqueness or local function of the farm. Does it just produce resources for its area? What lost traditions can be recycled? Which country is producing the most farms, and which is the most affected due to climate change?

Episode scenarios:

1. Peter travels to India, Australia, America, Brazil, Tanzania, Peru, France, and Japan to see how goat farming is changing livestock resources. Or Peter reports from India about 8 different farming practices local to the states.

2. Peter travels to Scotland, Canada, Iceland, South Africa, Chile, Egypt, Seychelles, and Taiwan to report on fish farming techniques and wild fish replenishment.
   Or Peter reports from China about 8 various farming practices including silk farming, rice paddies, wheat agriculture, energy farms, and how climate change and massive engineering projects are affecting local farming culture.

3. Peter travels to Mexico, Russia, Spain, Norway, Ghana, Namibia, New Zealand and Viet Nam to discover how local farms are offering global markets their wares.
Or Peter reports from the US about 8 different farms growing GM crops, alternative fuels, and transforming land into energy farms (wind, solar, tidal).

4. Peter travels to countries who farms are failing due to climate change and adaptations to survive or die. Or to those farms which have transformed themselves into Historical farms or into tourist attractions to survive.
Etc, etc.

Audience:
Audiences have warmed to new farming techniques and views from 'Jimmy's Food Farm' to Hugh Fearnley-Whittingstall at River Cottage programmes and also to the modern cooking techniques and food advocacy of Jamie Oliver. They are becoming more savvy and aware to food issues and land and animal welfare. **Around the World in 80 Farms** will be a unique modern guide to the changing face of the farm and what they have to do to survive the political, economic, and natural climate.

Around the World in 80 Farms will attract a youthful audience, eager for the travelogue-type experience while discovering or even re-discovering new food, energy, and farming practices around the world. For new and interesting ideas on future farmland use and where farming could be heading, come **Around the World in 80 Farms**.

End.

13/Apr/2019

Future Archaeology

Premise: Archaeology searches for past of humans, but what does the future of archaeology look like? We ask leading archaeologists for their views on where archaeology is going and what will the 21st century and beyond bring with the discoveries.

Channel:

USP: Informed speculation using some CGI and on-the-horizon technology detailing the new tools, techniques, and sites future archaeology will bring. Each show will aim to create and test new archaeological tools and techniques.

Talent:

Format:
In each of the four 60' programmes, the presenters will examine what new tools, technologies, sites, and theories will bring more to archaeology.

Content:
Episode 1: Extreme Archaeology – What will new geopolitical and global warming opportunities will present themselves? New sites in the frozen wastes? Will war or opening democracies help or hinder archaeology? What sites are in danger from desertification, urbanisation, jungle encroachment or rising seas and how can we detect or discover such sites, which could be lost forever? Middle East, Africa, and South America?

Episode 2: Techno Archaeology – What new technology will unlock the secrets of new and even old sites? Both in the field and post-excavation? We ask Archaeologists and inventors devise, build and test a new archaeological tool. But is lo-tech still better than hi-tech? Can we get more accurate dating techniques, especially for stone? Will archaeology be more CSI than Indiana Jones? What archaeological dream machine can they make – 3D printers, deciphering and translation devices, and archaeology apps?

An archaeology app displaying real-time positions of excavations, exhibitions, museums, and other matters of archaeology.

Episode 3: The New Archaeologists – How much more can we learn? Is 'old school' archaeology a thing of the past or will digging still be king versus non-destructive digs, caution versus risk.

Episode 4: Exo-Archaeology - New field or pipe dream? Trowelling on Mars, the Moon and beyond.

Episode 5: The Interactive Past: How will the spoils of archaeology be presented and interpreted? Will virtual museums and sites be created – building worlds from the mind into reality?

Audience:
Future Archaeology will attract those interested in archaeology, technology, and futurology. While Time Team and the ilk were rooted in the present Future Archaeology dares to present the future of archaeology and attract the archaeologists of the future. Viewers and casual viewers will be drawn in by the cutting edge of experience.

End.

08/Jun/2019

Sci-Fi Weekly

2020 vision
The last of my ideas so far and an evolving one. There is so much similar online content out there, I'd have to see how to make this relevant and different to all the others.

Premise: Online interactive geek and sci-fi presented fun.

USP: Fan presented discussions on all things sci-fi.

Channel: YouTube

Talent: Presenter: Ray Burke, rotating panel of guests and hosts. An on-set person monitoring social media for comments, questions, and 'live (geek) news'.

Format: 30'+ programmes (time limit can vary). Location to be determined. Set and props to be determined. Equipment required: Camera and/or iPad, microphones, tripods/gimbal stabalisers, lighting, video editing software.

Content: **Sci-Fi Weekly** is a weekly programme presented by non-experts and non-gatekeepers; fans like the audience who enjoy sci-fi and fantasy. **Sci-Fi Weekly** will be a televisual outlet rather than a blog/vlog or online news feed site.

Episode layout: The presenter(s) will interview fellow fans on their views of various sci-fi programmes, films, books, events, etc including favourites on genre, websites, social media, merchandise, personalities/celebrities, rumours, art, shout outs to other groups, cosplay, comic books/graphic novels, and forthcoming events and features. Sci-Fi Weekly will be an inclusive programme discussing sci-fi's affect on gender, race, and ethnicity.

Sci-Fi Weekly will also have quizzes, spolier alerts, call-ins/twitter and social media participation. One feature will be to invite experts such as police, insurers, medical staff, psychologists, etc to discuss how their profession would deal with real life superheroes, zombie attackers, and aliens.

Audience: **Sci-Fi Weekly** will garner a live studio audience and online subscribers of both males and females. The show will be PG rated/family-friendllly so children can watch with adults. **Sci-Fi Weekly** will be a gateway for those wishing to discover, discuss sci-fi/fantasy, and learn more about our unreal reality.

Subscribers: Sci-Fi Weekly will be a YouTube programme and will require subscribers for additonal funds along with advertising (e.g. Google ad sense), and manual advertising in the form of flyers and promos at events and online.

End.

Afterword

As mentioned in *Musings of an Infovore*, I have always endeavoured to be creative, a little non-conformist, and a free-thinker outside of the echo-chamber surrounding me. It's led me down some interesting paths and moulded me into the Infovore I am today.

Times have changed, interests have waxed and waned, and thus ideas have been compartmentalised and stored away for future use. My years of creativity, which have been presented in these two volumes, were distilled moments from my past and a path toward my future. There's so much to know and learn and so little time to do it. But I hope in some way, I have also inspired others so that my words have given rise to reflection, rage and revelation.

Social media has made unique idea creation and dissemination easier, but also made the competition fiercer both in sheer numbers and in criticism received. No wonder others hide their talents and others lash out in jealousy, rejection, and despair. But my advice would always be, if you don't try, you'll never know. Even if just for yourself, challenge yourself, create your own worlds and be proud of them. Creativity is Opportunity. So what are you waiting for? Be the next Infovore.

www.ingramcontent.com/pod-product-compliance
Lightning Source LLC
Chambersburg PA
CBHW070631310726
48982CB00001B/245

* 9 7 8 1 9 1 6 2 7 4 6 3 1 *